THE BOOK OF
ILSINGTON
•A PHOTOGRAPHIC HISTORY OF THE PARISH•

Dick Wills

Foreword by Rt Hon. Lord Tebbit of Chingford

Preface by Rt Hon. Lord Monro of Langholm

HALSGROVE

First published in Great Britain in 2000

British Library Cataloguing-in-Publication Data
A CIP record for this title is available from the British Library

ISBN 1 84114 060 0

HALSGROVE
PUBLISHING, MEDIA AND DISTRIBUTION

Halsgrove House
Lower Moor Way
Tiverton, Devon EX16 6SS
Tel: 01884 243242
Fax: 01884 243325
email www.halsgrove.com

Printed and bound in Great Britain by Bookcraft Ltd, Midsomer Norton

Contents

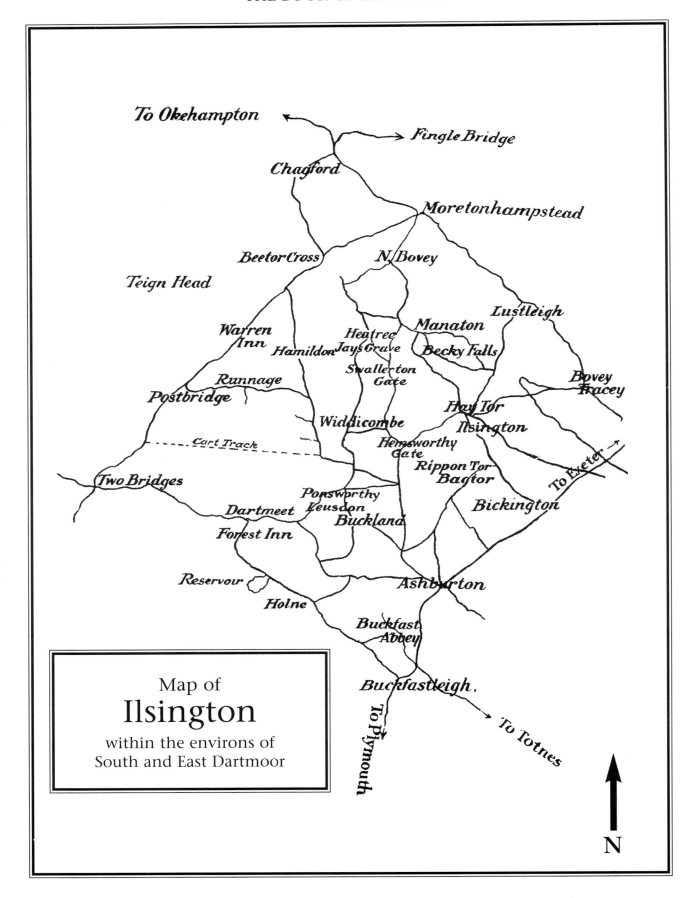

Map of
Ilsington
within the environs of
South and East Dartmoor

Foreword

by Lord Tebbit

The headlines of history, the Roman invasion, the Norman Conquest, Magna Carta, the Wars of the Roses, right through to the Battle of Britain, are the mountains of our historical landscape. But they are not the complete picture of the history of our people and country. They are macro-history and what is often forgotten or neglected is the micro-history of the lives and times of ordinary people – and some less than ordinary – in the villages and towns of England. Great decisions were taken in palaces but often they became so confused and muted as they were put into practice that everyday decisions were taken in parlours, even pigsties, and thus had more impact on the lives of the king's subjects, wherever they lived.

Uncovering the past is part of our understanding who we are and from whence we came. At one extreme archaeologists dig to discover our long-lost past. At the other extreme the book that Dick Wills has put together covers the more recent past, where photographs become the main source of our appreciation of former people and places. The Wills family is one of those threads which make up the history of Ilsington and which has given such resilience to this rural community. Dick Wills himself, like all good historians, has the instincts of a magpie, picking up and hoarding all manner of artefacts, stories, books, papers and photographs which might otherwise have been lost forever. Future historians may well be overwhelmed by the sheer amount of archive information available to them but Dick Wills has had to hunt down the material for this book - and his knowledge of the parish is all the more certain because of it.

I am always struck by how little life has changed in parishes like Ilsington. Our local Industrial Revolution, inspired by mining, had its affect, but growing industrialisation and urbanisation elsewhere in Britain left the parish untouched. It was the coming of the railways and the motor car which began to change rural Devon, and parish records which for centuries showed almost no marriages taking place outside the parish, now revealed a changing pattern in movement well beyond the familiar boundaries of Ilsington. In this book Dick Wills takes us from the settled years through to more turbulent modern times and his work is important in capturing the evidence of such changes.

Sadly my time in the parish is ending after only sixteen years so I have been part of that turbulent change, for which I have little affection. I shook off my time in its near namesake (but how different!), Islington, with no regrets, but I know that Dick Wills' history of the parish will not easily gather dust on my bookshelf for part of me will always be in Ilsington.

Norman Tebbit
Ilsington 2000

Acknowledgements

Firstly thanks are due to Marion Grant for the great help she has given to the author in providing the 'I Remember' sections in this book regarding her early life in Ilsington Village.

I would also like to thank the following for help given to me through the years in collecting parish and family history, and the photographs from which this book is compiled: John Somers Cocks, Bill and Peggy Ransom, Roger Nosworthy, Arthur and Lily Courtier, Aileen Carrett, Ed Williams, Les Manley, Lord Hector Monro, Connie Klinkenberg, Rob and Ann Parkinson, Roger Perkins, Bill Blinston, Lily Gilbert, Bob Cornish, Basil and June Philp, Ian Woodason, Val Williams, Karen Courtier, Harry Denley, Barry Squire, Derek Barber, Harry Shiels, Eddie Lee, Muriel Bunclark, Heather Edwards, John and Margaret Hendy, Laurence Keefe, John Benson, C.K. Croft Andrew, Pat Saunders, Aubrey and Dorothy Warren, May Honeywill, Robin Stanes, Robin Hood, Sydney Reed, Val Ransom, Bill Amery, Joyce Harlow, George Sealy, George and Yvonne Ware-Owen, Marianne Cross, Jack Wills, Jim Wills, Michael Wills, my father Sydney Wills, and many others.

DEDICATION

To all my family and the people of Ilsington past and present, and especially to my niece, Katie Wills 1978–1988, who did not live long enough to enjoy her birthright.

Preface

by Rt Hon. Lord Monro of Langholm

Ingsdon Manor was the home of the Monros for nearly a century. Had my Grandfather, Brigadier Seymour Monro not been killed on service in India in 1907 the estate might still have been in the family. I visited the house as a schoolboy in the 1930s and again after the war and realised at once its magnificent situation with its views out to Torbay.

Thanks to the kind help of Dick Wills, whom I have known for many years, I have been able to trace some of our history in Ilsington parish. The chapel in the church and the churchyard contain a number of family memorials and the Monro coat-of-arms in the lady chapel window is very similar to mine of today. The church also recalls the life of Anne Hale from whose family we inherited Ingsdon. We still use Hale among our family Christian names.

Perhaps more importantly for the parish Dick Wills' family and my own family worked together to establish two schools in the 1870s. They too were interested in Ilsington church, such a dominant and attractive feature of the village. I am sure Dick Wills' book will create much interest and will add important historical facts at the beginning of the new millennium.

Hector Monro
House of Lords, 2000

Narracombe Farm, home of the author, Dick Wills.

Introduction

by Robin Stanes - author of *The Old Farm* and *A History of Devon*

Dick Wills is the fourteenth generation of the Wills family to live and farm at Narracombe. This astonishing continuity, though not unique in Devon, must be a great rarity in today's rootless world and must add a dimension to a man's life. This shows in Dick's life and work

He was born in Ilsington and has lived there all his life, apart from a period at Allhallows school at Honiton and Rousdon, and another during World War Two when he was posted to India in the RAF. These periods widened his perspective well beyond the parish boundaries, but it is what lies within those parish boundaries that are his inspiration and interest. There can be little of Ilsington, its farms and fields, its church and its families and people that he is not aware of, and he has lived and farmed at Narracombe and done his civic duty in Ilsington for half a century. He has lived through and absorbed the great farming revolution of the 1930s and 40s that saw the end of the horse as motive power on the farm after millennia, the end, largely, of the hard hand-labour of hedge laying, hoeing, rick-making and muck spreading etc., and the substitution of the machine and chemistry for inherited knowledge and observation and, 'the best manure', the farmers foot. When Dick first farmed Narracombe there were four full-time employees, now there are none, on 300 acres!

Unlike most farmers Dick is immensely attracted by the past and by the evidence for it to be found everywhere in the landscape, on the map, and in family and village papers and documents, and in his own and other folks memories. A part of this lifelong accumulation of memories and photographs and knowledge are brought together in this book.

Robin Stanes
Payhembury 2000

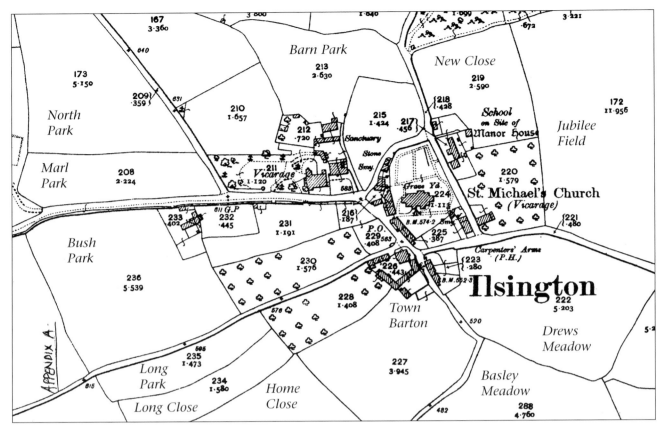

The village of Ilsington from an OS map c.1900.

Sanctuary Cross, Ilsington village c.1900. This was before the construction of the 'new road' in 1906, when the road to the left led only to Narracombe.

1 - Ilsington Village

Ilsington Village is situated around the parish church in a fairly central position of the parish. In earlier years it was known as 'Church Town' or simply 'Town', which made a former vicar complain when an old parishioner said he was going to Town, when he meant Ilsington Town and not London, which the vicar had first thought. Today we have the names Town Barton, Town Wood, Town Hill, and the recent Town Meadow to remind us of the old name.

Ilsington is an ancient settlement very likely dating from two or three centuries before the Norman conquest when a Saxon lord Merleswein owned it. By 1066 it had already a lot of land cleared from the ancient forest and scrubland, quite a feat when it all had to be done by hand and with primitive tools.

The first buildings would have been around the manor house, and this would have been where the first church was built on its present site, very likely a small thatched wooden or cob building, gradually enlarged and rebuilt through the centuries. The manor house was occupied for over a millennium, until 1825, when it became very dilapidated and eventually a quarry for any-one who wanted stones. It is interesting to note that its last inhabitants were the Southward family, whose descendants in America are still interested in Ilsington today.

Through the centuries the village thrived and was self-supporting. In the church registers and the later census returns, descriptions of villagers are given as farmers, butchers, bakers, tailors, miners, husbandmen, yeoman, moorstone cutters, millers, weavers, blacksmiths, carpenters, hewers of stone, shoemakers, masons, chapmans, quarrymen, cordwainers, thatchers, charcoal burners, woodmen and every trade needed to support a community. One main drawback was that the actual site did not have a spring of water. The main houses had their wells, but the cottagers had to rely on the potwater leat which ran down from Haytor in an open gutter, providing water to people and animals on the way. It got very polluted at times and, in the village, an open sewer when people could not be bothered to carry their buckets to their gardens. There was a spring of water in a field on the way to Simms Hill if they were particular, or the brook at Narracombe, but it all had to be carried uphill.

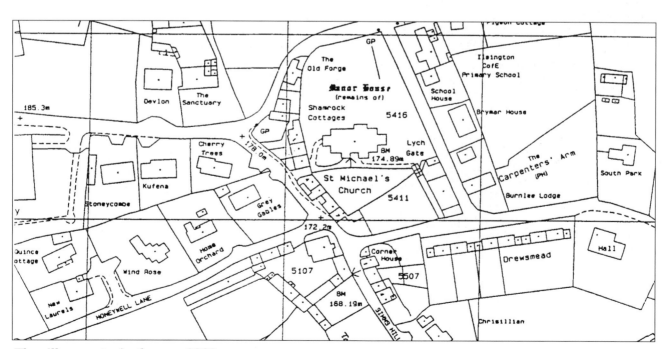

The village centre in the year 2000.

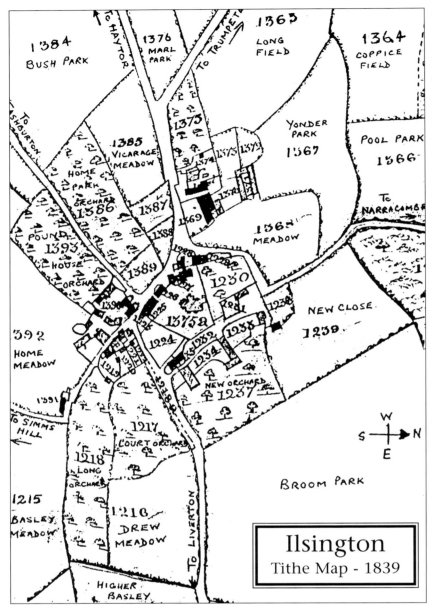

ILSINGTON TITHE MAP . 1839

the present Post Office stands; that 1218a was designated as 'The Addle Pool', the ditch where all the village drains were emptied manually (this ditch existed alongside the road until the Drewsmead houses were built); and that it appears 1237 and 1239, New Orchard and New Close, had been the ancient gardens of the Manor House. The Church did not stand on an island site as it does today but had the manor house and its grounds on its east side. This had just ceased to be used as the farm-house of Court Barton, and the two village farms of Court and Town Barton were now farmed together by my great-uncle Charles Corbyn Wills who also owned most of the cottages. Numbers not named on the map are: 1219 two cottages occupied by Robert Burn and Roger Poat; 1220 cottage, William Cumming 1221; cottage, Francis Blackler; 1222 two cottages, John Warren and another; 1223 garden; 1224 garden; 1225 three cottages, Joseph Courtier, Joseph Denley and another; 1226 cottage, William Cummings jun., owned by Jonas Mitchell; 1227 empty, late the Poor House; 1228 cottage, Joseph Kingwell; 1229 cottage, George Campion, blacksmith; 1230 Churchyard Orchard; 1231 garden; 1232 a plot; 1233 garden; 1234 barn, linhay and yard; 1235 Carpenters Arms, owned and occupied by William Northway; 1238 cottage and garden; 1369 Rectory House; 1370 garden; 1371 barn, stable and yard; 1372 garden, 1373 garden; 1374 Vicarage House, Rev. W.M.T. Paige; 1375 Vicarage Orchard; 1387 Vicarage garden; 1388 Rectory garden; 1389 Town Barton garden; 1390 farmhouse and buildings, etc. of Town Barton; 1391 cottage and smith's shop, Thomas Campion, blacksmith.

The Tithe Map and Schedule were the results of a survey by the Tithe Commissioners throughout the country to assess the value of all property for tithes to be paid in money instead of in kind. They name the owner and occupier of every house and the condition of every piece of land, including the name and size of every field and enclosure.

The Tithe Map of Ilsington is the earliest detailed map of the parish known to exist, and the adjoining extract from it shows the Ilsington Village of 1839 to be 'a village set among orchards'. Items of special interest to be seen from it are that no building then existed where

The Sanctuary was called The Rectory in the early part of the 19th century because it was part of the rectorial glebe of Ilsington and owned by the patrons of the living, the Dean and Canons of Windsor. Down through the years it has usually been called Sentry, simply the Cornish word for 'glebe'. Sanctuary is a corruption of that.

The heart of Ilsington village. An aerial photograph taken in 1961 showing the farm of Town Barton with barns intact and many productive vegetable gardens throughout the village. Shortly after this time new houses were built along Honeywell Lane and towards the vicarage.

Below: *A view of the village, Pinchaford Ball and Haytor Rocks, from a postcard c.1908. The picture is taken from Jubilee Field, where South Park is now built. Corn ricks stand waiting for threshing in the winter months. Note that the room above the lychgate has not been rebuilt. The newly built Haytor (Ilsington) Hotel stands above the trees and the church tower is without its coat of rough cast.*

Ilsington - 'The village in the Woods'. Ancient woodland of oak which was coppiced in the 18th and 19th centuries for charcoal and the leather industry. The last of the charcoal burners were the Southward family, last inhabitants of the then nearly derelict Ilsington Manor House. Employed by Charles Corbyn Wills up to about 1825, the places where charcoal was burnt in Town Wood can still be seen today.

The centre of the village, 1980. Medieval farming strips can still be seen in the right conditions in Town Barton Meadow. Narracombe Farm is visible in the distance on the right.

The village looking west, with Ramshorn Down in the middle distance and Denbury Hill further on. In the distance are Paignton, Brixham and Totnes, hidden by hills on the horizon.

The Vicarage was a building end on to the road. It had been rebuilt during the Rev. Jonathan Palk's incumbency, 1790–1825. In 1798 he had written 'I do not live in my Vicarage House as it is too ruinous to be inhabited or even repaired. As soon as my father, who is 84, enables me, I will rebuild it'. The Rev. Robert Lovett is reputed to have said that the Vicarage was not fit for a gentleman to live in when he came to Ilsington in 1867, and consequently built a new wing on to the older house which was demolished 60 years later. The present 'Old Post Office', 1226 on the Tithe map, owned by Jonas Mitchell had been built on 'a spott of ground' on which stood an old cottage called Rowells Cottage, by his grandfather John Soaper in 1790. The Cummings family and their descendants the Heathmans lived there until 1939.

The Church House, now St Michael's Cottages, backing on to the churchyard, became the parish poor house when laws passed at the beginning of the 17th century compelled the parish to maintain its poor people. Before this time it was the parish hall used for meetings and village activities, and also housed the church brew-house.

ILSINGTON VILLAGE

When the Rev. J. D. H. Patch came to Ilsington in 1908 the Ilsington (Haytor) and Moorland Hotels had just been built. Between them there were no houses except Lewthorn Cottages and Smokey Cross. The surface of the road was reasonably good as far as Lewthorn, but beyond it, it became very rough and nothing but a cart track until it joined the Bickington road at Smokey Cross. There was practically no traffic along it in the winter months except one or two farm and tradesmen's carts. In summer four-horse chara-bancs came from Newton Abbot and stopped for half an hour at the top of the New Road (opened in 1906) to rest the horses. Passengers meanwhile strolled about the village and visited the Church, where their offerings were a welcome addition to the Church funds.

As time went on and motor cars made their appearance, the surface of the road became very dusty, with the result that the stream or potwater running down the side became, after rain, the colour of pea soup and the villagers at Ilsington were unable to obtain any clear water for perhaps days on end.

It was obvious that some other water supply would have to be obtained and eventually the Lord-of-the-Manor granted the Newton Abbot Rural District Council permission to construct a reservoir at Haytor near the Quarries, and a piped water supply was obtained in 1914. At first there were merely stand-pipes outside the cottages, whose conditions were getting worse and worse and causing much anxiety as the owner, a Mrs Rowell of Torquay, was financially unable to do any extensive repairs. Eventually she accepted the purchase price put on them by the district valuer, and the RDC bought them and planned to demolish them all and build new council houses. Luckily at this time, Capt. C. H. Quelch retired from London and came to live in the parish, and with ministry grants, purchased them and was able to recondition them as they are today.

Simms Hill Cottages, Ilsington Village c.1900. Compare this with the photograph overleaf.

ILSINGTON VILLAGE

Simms Hills Cottages, 1990. Compare this with the earlier view below.

I REMEMBER...

How hard the women of the village worked, especially the ones with six or eight children, which was common in those days.

April began with the ritual of Spring Cleaning. The scrubbing brush was very much in evidence and everything that could be scrubbed was scrubbed! Curtains and bedspreads were washed and pillows were emptied of their feathers and the ticking washed. The the feathers were replaced. Blankets were washed, but not during the month of May, for the rhyme went 'Wash a blanket in May and you'll wash one of the family away!'.

Above: *Simms Hill Cottages with Mrs Philip Bickley standing at the door. I remember Mrs Bickley on her knees scrubbing the floor of St Michael's with a hand scrubbing brush, a bucket of cold water, and a tablet of red Lifebuoy soap.*

Right: *Another view of Simms Hill Cottages. At No.2 Mrs Commins had a small grocery shop in her kitchen. At No.4 the Honeywill family lived and kept their cobbler's shop.*

ILSINGTON VILLAGE

I REMEMBER...

I can remember seeing my mother standing on the table in our living room, washing the oak beams in the ceiling. And all this scrubbing and washing was done with hot water from big iron kettles which stood on the kitchen range. No washing machines, Rayburn stoves, gas or electricity in those days. Is it any wonder that people were considered old at sixty in those days? They were probably worn out.

Above: *May Wills outside Town Barton. Note the gutter which carried waste water down Simms Street.*

Above: *Ilsington Post Office and two of the three cottages at Town Barton Corner, c.1930.*

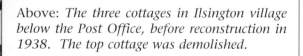

Above: *The three cottages in Ilsington village below the Post Office, before reconstruction in 1938. The top cottage was demolished.*

Left: *The Carpenters Arms. Thought to have been the farmhouse of Court Barton and which became a public house about 1816. Note the galvanised-iron-clad barn to the right, said to have been the tithe barn.*

ILSINGTON VILLAGE

Far left: *The church tower and the Old Post Office from Town Barton gateway.*

Left: *No.1 Simms Hill Cottage.*

Below: *A painting showing Ilsington village from the church entrance.*

Below left: *The road to Haytor from Ilsington, 1980.*

Right: *Joshua Courtier 1846–1907, and perhaps his two sons, Alfred and Henry, who were both killed in the First World War. Joshua and his brother, Charlie, both lost a leg in accidents, one a left leg the other the right, so they were able to wear one pair of boots between them. Note the riding steps against the building on the right. I remember these were made from old grave stones.*

ILSINGTON VILLAGE

Above: *Sanctuary Corner, 1980, showing the Old Forge on the site of the Blacksmith's Shop, and Shamrock Cottages.*

I REMEMBER...

Very few children possessed toys bought from a shop. Mr Commins, the blacksmith, used to produce an iron hoop with a handle (we called it a steer), and to be the owner of one of these hoops you would have to pay him a penny and take him a horse shoe, which you may find in a field, and sit by the smithy fire blowing the bellows while he made a hoop.

I think we were just as happy with our simple toys as the children of today with all the sophistication of the present age.

Left: *Shamrock Cottage, before reconstruction. The kitchen of the first cottage was about two feet lower then the road. The home of Mr and Mrs Sidney Roberts and, next door, Mr and Mrs Honeywill Snr.*

Below: *The Post Office, Ilsington c.1905. Note the granite shute on the left where the potwater was collected for domestic use (no piped water until 1914), and the gutter on the opposite side of the road for slopwater. Girls all wore white pinafores over their everyday clothes for special occasions, such as having their photograph taken! The boys wore well-patched knickerbockers and hobnail boots.*

ILSINGTON VILLAGE

I REMEMBER...

As there was no transport from the village except a bicycle (if you were fortunate enough to possess one) the butcher, baker, fishmonger and various other tradesmen, visited the village once or twice a week in their horse-drawn vehicles, bringing all necessary provisions.

The other way to get about was to walk. Even the elderly thought nothing of walking to Bovey Tracey to visit the doctor, six miles of hilly lanes there and back. Some young stalwarts would walk to Newton Abbot for a day out which was fourteen miles there and back, all up hill and down dale. For most, the walk to Newton fair was the only holiday they could expect in a year.

There was one other way of getting transport to Newton Abbot. Mr Sam Carpenter who was a farmer in the village, went to market every Wednesday in his horse and trap, and he could take two passengers with him. He would charge one shilling for an adult and sixpence for a child. As the average wage in those days was eighteen shillings a week, there were few takers. Aunt Anna with her comfortable income sometimes took me on this exciting journey.

Oh! the joy of sitting in the high trap on the padded seat, wedged between Mr Carpenter and Aunt Anna, bowling along the country lanes with the clip clop of the horses hooves ringing in my ears. Then the town, with the crowds of people, and the shops with so many exciting things to sell.

Top left: *St Michael's Cottages and the old barn and church tower.*

Top right: *With the vicarage (demolished 1934) and the Sanctuary in the background, a boy (possibly Jack Carpenter) waits with his horse and trap.*

Left: *Miss Alice Cummings (later Mrs Heathman), May Wills and Ronald Harris, of Sigford, on horseback outside Ilsington Post Office and shop.*

ILSINGTON VILLAGE

POSTAL INFORMATION.

ILSINGTON POST OFFICE:
Deliveries: 7.30 a.m., 6 p.m. (by calling at Office)-
Despatches: 9.40 a.m., 6.10 p.m.
Telegraph and Public Telephone.
Office closed Thursdays after 1 p.m.

HAY TOR VALE POST OFFICE:
Deliveries: 7.20 a.m., 6.10 p.m. (by calling at Office)-
Despatches: 9.35 a.m., 6 p.m.
Public Telephone.

CHURCH SERVICES.

SUNDAYS: H.C., 8 a.m.
Sung Eucharist, 11 a.m.
Evensong, 6.30 p.m. (3 p.m. in Winter)-
Children's Service, 3 p.m.
WEEK-DAYS: H.C. as announced.
SAINTS' DAYS: H.C. 8.15 a.m.

Top left: *Timetable for the Post Office and church services c.1930.*

Top right: *Ilsington Post Office and Stores were kept by Mrs Cumming and later by her niece, Mrs Alice Heathman. Here too, after 1909, was the telegraph office from where telegrams could be sent and received by Morse Code. The cottage next to the Post Office was demolished in 1938.*

Left: *The back of the three cottages below the Post Office. Note the slated lean-to.*

Left: *A view towards the church. Note again the granite shute of the potwater leat which carried water down from Haytor in an open gutter.*

ILSINGTON VILLAGE

I REMEMBER...

I vaguely remember being led by the hand of an older girl to the village school. The school consisted of two rooms, the little room and the big room. The former housed the infants of 4 to 7 year olds, and they were taught by Mrs Burnett, the head teacher's wife. In the big room Mr Burnett taught the rest, aged up to 14. There were about 20 children in the school.

At the age of 6 I remember being taught how to hem a handkerchief. The stitches had to be very small or they would have to be taken out and done again. My hands got hot and sticky as I tried to push a large needle through the course material, and the work got hot sticky and grubbier. I was terrified when Mrs Burnett overlooked my work. During this lesson she wore a thimble on her finger with which she would give me a sharp tap on the head and shout 'Out' which meant I was meant to take the stitches out and start again.

Present day standards would think this a useless exercise for a 5 to 6 year old.

Quite rightly so!

Above left: *Just out from school and, finding a photographer on the scene, Ilsington schoolchildren posing for the camera include Hilda Roberts, Ronald Commins, Winnie Tarr, Margaret Tarr and Charlie Heathman.*

Left and centre: *It is interesting to compare these two pictures. The first was taken in 1905 and the second after restoration of the cottages, c.1940.*

ILSINGTON VILLAGE

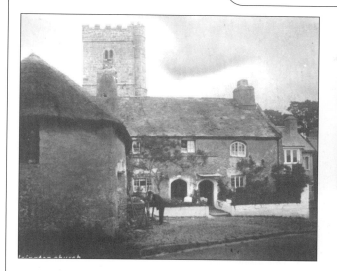

Various views of St Michael's Cottages before and after restoration.

Top Left: *The Cottages in 1925 showing the Old Barn to the left.*

Above: *The three cottages of St Michael's, 1935. No.1 was home of the Strawbridge family, in No.2 lived Mr and Mrs Tom Tarr and family, and in No.3 Mr and Mrs William Ball.*

Left: *St Michael's Cottages c.1930. The right-hand dwelling was once the parish brew house and, for a short time, the Church House Inn. Notice the line along the facing wall where the lean-to once existed and where the upper part of the brew house was entered. Originally the whole building was the Church House and, later, the left hand end was the Parish Poor House.*

Left: *The cottages a year after their restoration by Captain Quelch in 1938. All these cottages could well have been demolished if he had not undertaken the task after they had been declared unfit for habitation, by Newton Abbot Rural District Council.*

ILSINGTON VILLAGE

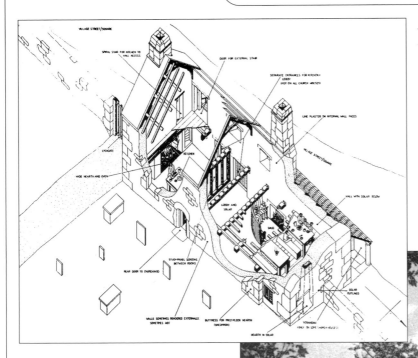

A theoretical reconstruction of St Michael's Cottages, formerly the Church House, Ilsington c. 1600.

Below: *Outside the Sanctuary, with the church, St Michael's cottages and the Old Barn. A boy (possibly Jack Carpenter) sits on the pavement with his dog.*

Below: *The Sanctuary, 1955, with the newly-built bungalow on the site of the old vicarage which had been demolished in 1934.*

Right: *Winter 1952 and snow clads the rooftops of Shamrock and St Michael's cottages. The children with the sledge are Anthony Klinkenberg, Gwen Northway, Margaret Wills and Geoffrey Klinkenberg.*

ILSINGTON VILLAGE

The church with Shamrock Cottages and, on the left, the Old Forge.

Left: *A view from the church tower looking up the Haytor road.*

Below left: *Looking down the lane past St Michael's Cottages.*

Below: *Steam roller outside the Carpenters Arms in 1992.*

ILSINGTON VILLAGE

Above: *Town Barton farmhouse with Alan Wheelhouses' steam engine under cover in the foreground. This farmhouse was rebuilt after a fire burnt down the former thatched dwelling in 1870. Its owner, in the 1990s was Sydney Reed, a former local veterinary surgeon.*

I REMEMBER...

Town Barton farmyard was one of my favourite haunts. Chickens, ducks, turkeys, pigs and a collection of cats roamed around. The cats lived in barns and kept the rats at bay.

If I saw Mr Redstone returning from his work in the fields with the cart horses Prince and Prance, I would be waiting for him. 'Here you are, Curly,' he would say as he released Prince from the cart 'take him to water.'

He knew Prince was my favourite. Although I was only about 8 years old, and small for my age, I had no fear of this enormous, gentle animal. The top of my head wouldn't have reached his nose!

Left: *The road to Haytor from Ilsington, 1930. The old vicarage was then still standing but it was demolished in 1934 and a new vicarage built in the garden. Note the cobbled pavement.*

Left below: *A photograph given by Rosemary Brown whose father ran a company, Rockey's of Torquay. This shows the firm's outing to Dartmoor in the 1920s. It was not noticed until recently that the picture was actually taken in Ilsington.*
The triangle in the centre of the picture is a yellow AA village sign.

2 - The Church and Methodism

ILSINGTON PARISH CHURCH
'A large building with a great surprise' - Pevsner

There have been numerous articles and booklets written about St Michael's parish church, Ilsington through the years, and I will try in this book to concentrate on those points which have been neglected or not so well known.

The present church as we now see it chiefly reflects the building which took place at the end of the 15th Century, but there was very likely a church on this spot some 500 years before that, when the Saxon Manor was first carved out of the ancient scrub and woodland. We know that a Saxon Lord called Merleswein held the manor before 1066, and that another called Peadington held the land at one time as part of a large estate. We also know at the time of the Domesday survey of 1087 the Norman lord, Ralf Pagnell, had an acre of meadow and pasture, 2 leagues and 8 furlongs in length and width, with 5 cattle, 40 sheep and 23 goats, with 22 villagers, 6 smallholders and 7 slaves.

The first written records of the church date from about 1187 when the Bishop of Exeter granted the advowson of Ilsington church to the Prior and Canons of Plympton, which they owned until 1338 when Bishop Grandisson of Exeter assigned it to his newly founded collegiate church of St Mary, Ottery. At the Reformation it was granted to the Dean and Canons of St George's, Windsor Castle, who still own it.

From the Saxon period until the end of the 14th century, Ilsington church gradually grew. First from being a wooden and cob structure with a thatched roof, to a small stone-built one, until the time came when the parish became more wealthy, through tin mining and woollen and cloth trades, and the parishioners wanted something better for the Glory of God, and to show off to their neighbours. It took time, but ended up with a new tower some seventy feet high, two new chapels on either side of the chancel, a nave separated from two side aisles by ten granite arcades supported on slender pillars, two transepts north and south, a new porch, a new richly carved

St Michael's parish church, Ilsington, from the south, 1920.

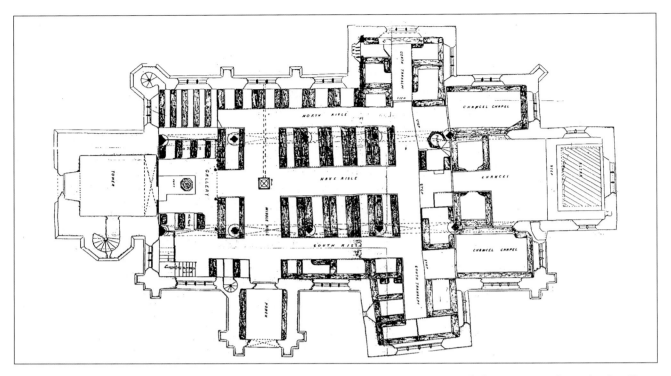

A plan of Ilsington church showing the seating arrangement prior to 1884, with box pews and a raised gallery at the back with choir and organ. Note the alignment of the south transept.

screen, and a spectacular roof and ceiling, comprising two Devonshire barrel-roofs joining in a central boss. Dr Pevsner in his book *The Buildings of England* notices the unusual roof array of Ilsington and the great surprise it gives on entering the church.

This major reconstruction can be dated after 1485 from the central boss which depicts a lion (the lion of England representing King Henry VII) standing over a vanquished white boar or hog (the emblem of Richard III) representing the Battle of Bosworth field. Around the edge of the boss are alternately the roses of Lancaster and York; signifying the end of the Wars of the Roses.

No doubt this rebuilding took several years to complete and it seems that the south transept was the last part to be completed, for the south wall contains a large perpendicular window, different to the others in the church – very spectacular, especially viewed from a distance. The south transept is also slightly out of line with the rest of the building, no great worry to medieval builders, and giving a sense of quaintness. Indeed Ilsington church has grown over the centuries, and its beauty is in its various architectural styles.

In Puritan times the whole church was plastered with layers of lime-wash and white paint and the colouring of carvings and the painting of saints on the screen were obliterated. When in the early 19th century the white colouring was scraped away, so went the ancient paintings and colours. In 1884 the box pews were replaced by modern ones and the choir gallery at the back of the church, which held the choir and organ, and before that the village orchestra, was demolished. The screen also lost its rood loft and the fan vaulting which supported it.

In my time as churchwarden several windows which contained green, blue, yellow and red cathedral glass have been replaced by clear leaded panes which let in the sunshine and give a view of the local countryside. Electricity for light and heating have replaced the oil lamps and coke-fired stove.

THE CARTOUCHE

In the north transept of Ilsington church there is a cartouche tablet, a wall monument common in the 17th and 18th centuries. It is to the memory of Rev. Philip Nanson's mother-in-law and reads: 'In memory of Sarah daughter of Francis Duncombe of Broughton in the county of Bucks. and relict of William Paynter D.D., formerly Rector of Exeter college in ye University of Oxford. She dyed in ye year of our Lord 1721 of her age 77. Those who knew her best, valued her most.'

Left: *St Michael's church interior showing the rood screen and crucifix and the wooden barrel roof of the chancel.*

Right: *The pulpit was made for the 1884 restoration, the upper part reflecting the carving of the screen. It covers at least one of the ancient ledger stones.*

Above: *The font is ancient and typical of moorland churches. Very likely it is the oldest artefact in the church.*

Above: *This interior view, looking towards the chancel, shows the slender pillars of granite, made in one piece, and the 15th century rood screen. The crucifix has now been taken off the screen and hangs from the roof timbers, while the wooden barrel roof has been plastered and the beams coloured.*

Left: *The nave and chancel. Note the organ in the north chancel which was the Bagtor Chapel before the 1884 restoration.*

LEDGER STONES IN CHURCH

There are several ledger stones in the floor of Ilsington Church, some of which were removed and put in different places at the time of the major restoration in 1884. The original ones were of 16th century vicars, in the chancel, and of members of the Lords of the Manor families in the Ilsington, Bagtor, Ingsdon and Colesworthy parts of the church, that is the north transept, north chancel chapel, south chancel chapel, and south transept respectively. The other prominent members of the parish were buried in the aisles mainly between 1635 and 1727.

Interesting epitaphs include:

Here lies Thomas Ford of Bagtor, knight who died on 27.3.1610. 'Faith on his brow, grace in his face, orderd in in his affairs, honesty in his breast, a pious mind, a joyful heart, of good hope, generous, giving his soul to God, giving his body to the dust. To the world a lamentable loss: but life with God.'

Here lies the body of Thomas Pomeroy of Engesdon Knight. Died 18.4.1610,, the 61st of his life. 'Behold King of Kings, you gave the royal fruit Pomeroy and you pluck it, for he who bears the fruit, let him reap it. Life is the way to death, and death is the gateway to life. That death which took my life, to me was life.'

John and his wife Mary Nosworthy of Sigford, who were buried at the same time on one day 12.3.1635. (John was a churchwarden and my 8 times great grandfather – author).

The recumbent figure in the north transept is thought to be either a Dinham or a Fissacre Lady of the Manor from the adjoining manor house.

The grave in the north aisle is of Elizabeth Ford, died 1629, wife of Thomas Ford of Bagtor and daughter of Lord Chief Justice Popham of Huntworth, Somerset. This is the grave which was chipped by a horse's shoe when it was stabled in the church during the very cold night of 9 January 1646 after the Royalist flight from the Battle of Bovey Heath during the Civil War. It is said the horses were restless and one stamped a piece out of the stone, which can still be seen. The soldiers and horses did not linger long and at first light made off towards Ashburton; when Cromwell's men arrived on the scene they were gone.

A PROBLEM UNSOLVED

Look at the floor of Ilsington Church a few feet from the south-east corner of the plinth on which

The north transept in St Michael's showing the recumbent figure of a Lady of the Manor, and the Wills' memorial window erected by George Wills of Narracombe in memory of his wife and two sons who died in 1860, 1870 and 1872.

Fragments of the inscribed stone on the floor of Ilsington church near the font.

the font stands, and you will see an irregular bluish black stone with some peculiar marks inscribed on it. It has been worn nearly smooth by countless feet walking over it, and it is in a vulnerable position today. It is obviously very ancient and but a fragment of its original self.

On 28 June 1793, a letter was written to the editor of the *Gentleman's Magazine*, Mr Sylvanus Urban, and signed by one 'Vicarius', probably the vicar of Ilsington, the Rev. Jonathan Palk. This letter was duly published in the magazine for July 1793 and read:

The three enclosed figures represent the fragments of a stone which are laid in different parts of the church at Ilsington in Devonshire. There are two or three other small fragments in the same pavement, but these are most wrought. This stone which is unlike to any taken from the neighbouring quarries appears to me to have been meant to commemorate a more than common person, as there is no other stone of superior quality, and but one of the same quality in the whole pavement and that commemorates a vicar interred here in 1539. An explanation may throw light upon some other remnants of antiquity in the same church.

One of the three engravings printed with the letter shows the fragments to be seen at Ilsington today. Even 207 years ago the stone was badly worn but parts of two words in Old English lettering can be distinguished on one side. The other two engravings show two smaller fragments which have now disappeared and again, on one of these, part of a word can be discerned.

'Vicarious' was slightly wrong when he said there was only one similar stone in the church, there are two. One commemorates the Rev. Hugh Bruseigh who died in 1532 and is situated in the chancel: the other, now badly worn and illegible, is also near the font above the grave of Elizabeth

Ford who died in 1628. This is the Royalist horse-shoe stone. It is interesting that all three stones have similar lettering on them.

A reply to 'Vicarious' was published in the August 1793 issue of the *Gentleman's Magazine* from a correspondent 'D.H.' who wrote: 'May not the fragments in Ilsington church belong to the tomb of William Beansi or Bransi or some such name, who was perhaps vicar of the church. The initials of his name W.B. are on each side of the shaft of the cross.' One of the words could be Beansi or Bransi, but where D.H. saw the initials W.B., I do not know, unless it was on another fragment of stone not illustrated. Similarly I do not agree that the word which D.H. took to be 'William' is definitely that.

Unless further evidence is found I do not think we will ever know whom the stone is meant to commemorate. I will however make a few suggestions. Could it be William Bousquyer, vicar of Ilsington, 1562–1577 who it is recorded was buried at Ilsington? Or a William Bruseigh, or Brusi, perhaps a relation of the Rev. Hugh Bruseigh, buried in the church? Looking at the condition of his tombstone I should say the unknown one is far older.

MARRIAGE REGISTERS

During the 58 years from 1754–1812, 354 weddings took place at Ilsington, just over six a year. Of the 354 bridegrooms signing the marriage register during that period, 187 of them, or nearly 53 per cent wrote their own signature, but the remainder used a mark to sign, and so can be considered illiterate. From the 354 brides, only 111 of them or just over 31 per cent were able to sign their name. This may be a little unfair to the ladies however, for during the time the Rev. Alexander Laskey was curate, from 1754–1771, the bride was required to sign her new surname.

The altar c.1905, shortly after the reredos was given to the church by Rev. Percy Wise. Note the detail on the 15th century screen, the lower panels of which once contained paintings of the saints.

Whereas she might have practiced her maiden name, perhaps she was not aware she was expected to write her new name, especially in front of her husband and new in-laws!

Most weddings were by banns, but 37 of them paid extra for a marriage licence, and did not have to suffer the indignity of having one's name called out three times in church. It was necessary to travel to Exeter to get the licence, and very often couples got married at the nearest available church in Exeter, before returning home. It is interesting to note the majority of weddings took place between Ilsington parishioners. The most popular 'foreigners' were from Ashburton (9 bridegrooms and 9 brides), Bovey Tracey (6 grooms and 5 brides), and Bickington (7 grooms and 3 brides). Then a big drop with Highweek next (5), Kingsteignton, Widecombe, Hennock, Ipplepen, Broadhempston, and Wolborough 3 each, Kingskerswell, Staverton, Buckland in the Moor and Lustleigh 2, and Moreton, Manaton, Christow, Dean Prior, Woodland, Stoke-in-

Teignhead, Teigngrace, South Brent, Abbotskerswell, Dunsford, Buckfastleigh, Berry Pomeroy, Lympstone, Launceston, and South Hill (Cornwall) one each.

People living temporarily in Ilsington at the time of their marriage are called sojourners, and during this period there were 113 of these, 68 bridegrooms and 45 brides. Presumably they were mostly working in the parish as apprentices.

No fewer than 30 members of the Bowdon family were married during the period, followed by 23 Taylors, 22 Laskeys and 21 Rowells. Families with more than 10 weddings are, Leaman 17, Paddon 16, Coleman 13, Wills and Honeywill 12 each, Campion and Eales 11, and Ford and Coysh 10.

One name which occurs as a witness to the weddings for the whole of the period is Isaac Ford. Father and son of the same name they were Parish Clerks. In the main the officiating ministers were Alexander Laskey curate, 1754–1771, Courtney Pierce curate 1771–1777, Thomas Compton curate 1778–1789, and Jonathan Palk, vicar 1789–1812.

Studying the registers, patterns can be seen to take shape through the years, thus 1759 can be called the Broadhempston Year, for in that year two brides and a bridegroom came from there, followed by a bridegroom from Staverton the next year. I wonder what the attraction was!

The controversial decorated reredos behind the altar which some people would, at the time of writing, like to see removed. Designed by T.H. Lyon of Middlecott and erected in memory of his sister, Caroline, by her husband Canon Percy Charlton Wise of Adelaide.

Left: *View of St Michael's and the church cottages in 1950, taken from the strip gardens which are jointly owned by several cottages.*

Below: *St Michael's church from the south.*

Above left: *There is a small room above the porch with a narrow stone staircase from the interior of the church. It is said to have been the bedroom of the travelling priest who went from church to church in pre-Reformation days.*

Left: *The old Wills' family graves on the east side of the church. There is something of a mystery concerning the quoin stones in the chancel wall which are made of red sandstone. Why this and not local granite which could easily be obtained at Haytor? The chancel is the oldest part of the church, perhaps built in the 12th century or earlier. When the plaster was removed from inside in 1999 the walls were seen to be chiefly built of small slate stones.*

The south porch showing three niches above the door. The central one contained, as now, the Blessed Virgin Mary with her lily and thorn emblems on either side, and with the letter MXT a fleur de lys and an R – the petitions from the Litany of Loretto. The left hand niche has S and A on either side, showing it once sheltered St Anne (mother of the Virgin), but the letters on the right hand side have completely disappeared.

THE STATE OF CHURCH PROPERTY IN 1727

The Rev. Philip Nanson, vicar of Ilsington, from 1715 to his death in 1739 compiled a terrier or inventory of church belongings in 1727.

The Vicarage House is built partly with slate stones and partly with moor-stones (granite) and covered partly with reed (thatch) and partly with shingles. It consists of twelve upper rooms, including closets all floored with boards and ceiled, and three of the said rooms are half wainscoted. It consists also of twelve lower rooms, all ceiled or lathe and plastered, except one which is under the Parsonage House (as the Sanctuary was then called, showing that the two houses were then joined together). One of the said rooms, viz. the parlour, is floored with boards and half wainscoted.

There is a barn there 40 ft. in length, and a linney adjoining on the east side 32 ft. in length, and a Necessary House (toilet) at the north end of the mansion house.

The Glebe is $7^{1/4}$ acres, according to an old terrier drawn up by the Rev. Robert Dove, vicar, and John Bowdon and William Wotton, churchwardens in 1636. The land which was then all enclosed contained the church Litten (Churchyard) $^{1/4}$ acre; Vicarage, garden and orchard 1 acre; Swine Park 30 acres; Down Park 18 acres; Broom Park 5 acres; Middle Park 5 acres; Higher Marl Park $2^{1/2}$ acres; Middle Marl Park 2 acres; Lower Marl Park 1 acre; Meadow 1 acre; North Park 3 acres; Long Marl Park 1 acre; Pool Park 1 acre.

Swine Park is divided into four fields, two arable and two furze ground and adjoins Coxland on the south side. Widdicombe's tenement is on the west and the highway on the north and east. Down Park is divided into five fields, all arable ground, and adjoins Honeywell on the south, and the highway on the other sides. Broom Park, Middle Park, Higher and Middle Marl Park (all arable ground) and the Meadow are all contiguous and are bounded by the vicarage barn and Cowses tenement on the east, and by highways on the west and both sides. Lower Marl Park, arable ground is bounded on the north by the highway and other by Mr Charles Corbyn's land (Town Barton).'

North Park and Long Marl Park, the former furze and the latter arable, adjoin each other and are bounded by the highway on the east and south sides and by Mr John Drake's land on the west and north. Pool Park, arable ground, is bounded by Narracombe on the north, and Court Barton on the east, and Sentry ground on the south and west sides. The Glebe has a right of common appertaining to it for all sorts of cattle, and it is not limited to any certain number of cattle of any sort.

The fences of the Church Litten are stone walls, repaired when there is occasion by a Parish Rate. There is one timber tree on the Glebe, an oak in the Meadow, worth 15 shillings and ten elms in the Church Litten worth 15 shillings a piece, and no others.

The agricultural state of some of the fields in 1727 is interesting. Most are known by the same names today, and some which are quite flat and workable were then covered with furze. But the fact that they were then enclosed, shows that they had been in a better state of cultivation at some earlier time. On the other hand Pool Park, next to

Donkey Trot Hill, which everybody knows as being 'as steep as the roof of a house,' was arable in 1727.

The terrier is also valuable for the reason that it gives the names of owners of neighbouring lands at the beginning of the 18th century. John Drake owned the land now occupied by the Ilsington Hotel and the land behind it. Apparently this was inherited from Catherine Ford, daughter of Sir Henry Ford, who married John Drake of Bystock, and was awarded 'the High Rate of Ilsington and Bagtor and other properties in Sigford and Ilsington' after the Chancery suit on the will of Sir Henry.

Lower Marl Park, an isolated field on the south side of Honeywill Lane, long and narrow, a remnant of the open field system, was surrounded by Town Barton land of Charles Corbyn, the last member of that old Ilsington family. Again the statement that the Glebe had an unlimited right of common, would not be acceptable today.

SALE OF GLEBE

The easiest way of old to hold property and to raise interest for the church, was the acquisition and holding of land. It was safe, not subject to be 'where rust or moth can corrupt or thieves break in and steal.' The Glebe was part of the endowment of a church and its rent was part of the incumbent's stipend.

Swine Park from time immemorial was part of the Glebe of Ilsington. Possibly it could have been given by an owner of Bagtor or Sigford Manor in whose manor it would have been. It was called Swinepath. That it was part of the Glebe is confirmed by the terriers. Those of the early 17th century give the impression that it was one large field, but the terrier of Rev. Nanson in 1727 states that it is divided into four fields, 2 arable and 2 furze ground 'and adjoins Coxland Tenement on the south, Widdecombe Tenement on west and ye Highways on the other sides.'

The household of Dr T.H. Braim, vicar of Ilsington 1875–1879 outside the vicarage. Left to right: *Miss Eleanor Braim; Mrs Caroline Braim (vicar's wife); Mrs Vincent (housekeeper); Dr T.H. Braim; Rev. J.S. Shields (curate); Miss Amy Braim and Lewis Heale (gardener).*

Left: *The vicarage from the south side – Vicarage Meadow. The west side of the house (west wing) was built for Rev. Robert Lovett when he came to Ilsington in 1867. He said the older part (built by Rev. Jonathan Palk about 1800) 'was not fit for a gentleman to live in.' He wintered in Torquay and employed a curate at Ilsington. In 1869 Neville Lovett was born at Ilsington, later to become Bishop of Salisbury.*

Above: *The entrance gates to the vicarage from the Ilsington–Haytor road in 1920. The thatched summer house can just be glimpsed on the left. Note the oil lantern on the gatepost.*

Above: *Family and staff of the Braim's who followed Rev. Lovett as residents of the vicarage. Dr Thomas Henry Braim (seen standing by the front door) is the author's great Grandfather.*

Above: *The vicarage seen from the road. The left-hand side was built for the Rev. Robert Lovett 1867–1875, the right-hand side by the Rev. Jonathan Palk 1790–1825.*

Left: *The conservatory and the east wing of the vicarage which was finally demolished in 1934, just 67 years after the new wing was built.*

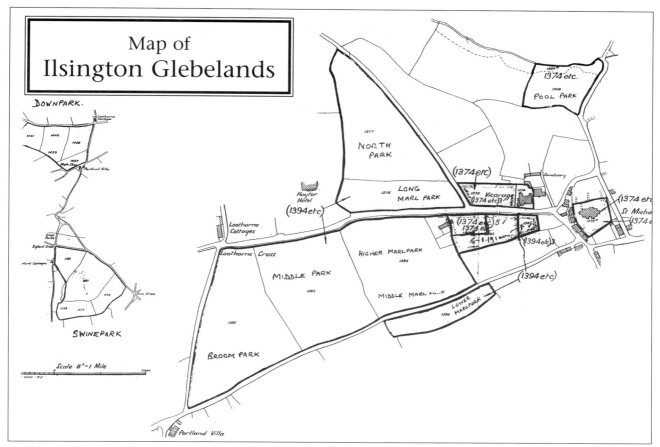

Map of
Ilsington Glebelands

In 1920 the Glebe lands were sold, and again Swine Park was sold in 1953 to the tenants Mrs and Mr L. Dymond. Sold again in 1977 it was split 24 acres to Mr S. Mann of Widecombe and 14 acres to Mr Crossman.

LISTED TOMBSTONES

Thomas Ford's grave with the date of death given in Roman numerals

There are eleven listed tombstones in the churchyard, nine of which are chest tombs or parts of them and two headstones.

Chest tombs are shaped like a chest or table and were popular with fairly well-off families at the latter part of the 17th century; the ones at Ilsington generally date from 1642 to 1686, there is one late one of 1759, and the two gravestones are dated 1677 and 1702.

Gravestone in the churchyard with the church cottages before they were restored in 1938.

There are very few stones earlier than 1750. Before that date very few graves were marked and when one thinks that there have been burials around the church since the first church, there must be many thousands of unmarked graves there.

The most interesting of the listed tombstones are:

No.333. Thomas Ford of Sigford. There is no date of his death, but the answer is in the form of a chronogramme in which the capital letters (here underlined) of his epitaph are added together in Roman numerals: 'DORMIO ET VT SPERO CINERES SINE LABE RESVRGENT' 500+ 1000+1+5+100+1+1+50+5 = 1663

No.388 Headstone with a skull and crossbones engraved on it. Elizabeth the wife of Stephen Laskey died 1702.

No.448 A thick granite headstone. Mary Bound buried 1677. 'It was desired by her who Iyeth here interred until the Resurrection, that her bones should not be moved.'

Other listed gravestones are:

231a Sibyll Southcote of Yarner 1674.

237a Edward Ford 1665.

238 Edward Ford of Sigford 1674.

281 Grace Furlong 1686.

323 George and Agnes Hart 1642.

361 Mary Codnor 1672.

373 Ambrose & Gregory Campion 1675 and 1673.

409 Eliza Weager 1759.

INSCRIBED AND CARVED STONES

During the 1883 restoration of Ilsington church the floor was relaid and it is known that two important stones were taken away from the church by the builders. One became a bridge across a stream at Cadewell, Torquay, and is now in the museum of the Torquay Natural History Society in Babbacombe Road. It is a stone which formerly had a prominent place in the church in the centre aisle and on it is engraved a cross with the letters W.B.

Another stone, described by Les Manley to be like an old-fashioned coffin lid with mouldings, fell off the carriers cart at Exeter Cross where it lay for many years, eventually used as a drain. When the road was widened about 1924 it was buried under rubble, where presumably it still lies.

A granite stone from the Ilsington Manor House, shaped like an overmantel of a fireplace, served as a bridge at the gate of the present

Ilsington Post Office until the 1980s when it was covered with tarmac.

Again loads of stone and rubble from the demolition of the west wing of the old vicarage in 1934, which contained carved granite mullions and arches from Ilsington Manor House, were used as hardcore for the machinery workshop at Rixey Park near Chudleigh Knighton. I managed to save a few lorry loads and the carved stones I saved are at Narracombe. Others were found in Town Barton farmyard and were built into the walls of Sydney Reed's new house (Ash House), and there are some at Barnlea, Pigeon Cottage (John and Linda Smith), and the gateways of Liverton Farm and Ingsdon Manor.

HEADSTONES

Unusual inscriptions include:

Elizabeth Smith, wife of George Rowell 1842.
How loved, how valued once, avails thee not.
To whom related, or by whom begot.
A heap of dust alone remains of thee,
'Tis all thou art and all the proud shall be.

Michael and Mary Rowell, 1805.
O see what death can do: it call for we,
Tomorrow may call for you.
Our name above you see
Prepare for Death and follow we.

Thomas Mortimore 1820, aged 27.
The world to me lost all the power to please,
I was afflicted with a slow disease.
Physicians and their skill were all in vain,
Till God was pleased to ease me of my pain,
And at the judgement day I hope to rise,
And with my Saviour live beyond the skies.

THE ILSINGTON SCHOOLROOM DISASTER
SEPT.1639

It is recorded in the church registers that on Tuesday 17 September 1639 an accident occurred at Ilsington which would be remembered for centuries to come. There was a building over the west lychgate, as there is today, which was used as one of the small schools of the parish, catering for about 30 boys, and run by Hannibal Corbyn. The day was wet and windy and 17 boys had remained at home. At about 11.00 am when the children were preparing to go home for their midday meal, a woman, taking no doubt a short cut through the

Above left: *The west lychgate with the statue of St George (part of a First World War memorial), and the Brasparts plaque (presented by the people of Brasparts, a Brittany town with which Ilsington is twinned). The lychgate and room above were designed by T. H. Lyon of Middlecott and built in 1910, replacing the schoolroom which collapsed in 1639.* Above right: *The south lychgate, photographed in 1980. Circles and shallow holes have been scratched in the eight granite steps by generations of children playing marbles. In 1997 a new cobbled area was laid to the road by the Dartmoor National Park.* Below: *These two oak posts supported the main entrance gate from 1870–1906 after the vestry room was demolished. When the new room was built they were converted into posts to hold a large oil lamp at the porch entrance. Rotten, they were removed in the 1960s.*

churchyard, went through the heavy oak gate and let it slam behind her. Before she had gone some 6 yards, the whole building collapsed, its side walls falling outwards and the roof to the floor. The south wall containing the fireplace and chimney remained intact. The original account says

'Not a stick, stone or pin of the original room remained in place.'

Four boys fell into the churchyard, one into the village street, and the rest were buried in the rubble of the building, except one boy who ran into the chimney of the hearth, where he remained unhurt.

Present at school when the building fell: Hannibal Corbyn (school master). David Leere, Thomas Leere, John Leere, Henry Leere (brethren). Thomas Smerdon, Thomas Corbyn, John Crerose, John and Humphry Degon (brothers), Stephen Tyler, Bartholomew Potter, Thomas Potter, John Michelmore, John Ford, John Stancombe, Hannibal Satterly and John Leate.

THE CHURCH BELLS

There are at present six bells in the Church Tower:

1. Treble. Note E. diameter 27" weight 4 cwt-lqtr-17lb, cast by Gillett and Johnston, of Croydon in 1926. Inscribed: Chas C. Cox (capt) Lewis Clark, William Redstone, Alf Head, Oliver Roberts, Fred Derges, Wm. Cox, Eli Bourne, Sidney Roberts, Jim Harvey (ringers). J. D. H. Patch, Vicar

2. Note D. 29" weight 5cwt-0qtr-14. Was the old treble bell. Inscribed: 'When I begin, then all strike in.' Made by T. Bilbie in 1797. Recast in 1870 as it was then cracked, by Mears of London. William Rowell and Thomas Widger (churchwardens).

3. 1828. Made by William and Charles Pannell of Cullompton. Charles Corbyn Wills and John Rowell (churchwardens).

4. Made by T. Bilbie in 1797. Samuel Nosworthy and John Rowell (churchwardens).

5. Made by T. Bilbie in 1797. Inscribed: 'God Save the King'.

6. The Tenor. 41½" diameter. 14¾ cwt. Made by Thomas Bilbie in 1797. Samuel Nosworthy and John Rowell (churchwardens).

In 1947 the six bells were rehung on a new steel frame by Gillett and Johnstone of Croydon and were taken down during the exceptionally cold spell of February that year.

BELLRINGING

One of the first entries in the old account book kept by the Ilsington churchwardens is in 1779 stating that half a crown has been paid to the ringers for ringing the bells 'on the taking of the Spanish Fleet.' This must have been during the American War. In those days, and for many years later, the ringers were paid five shillings annually for ringing the bells on the King's Coronation Day, or as succeeding churchwardens called it 'The King's Crown Nation Day,' and the Fifth of November. There is no record of any payments for ringing on other days. After the ringing of the 5th November 1795, the bells became silent. What caused it is unrecorded but at least four bells had to be re-cast and a 7d Church Rate bringing in £50.13.10d was levied in 1796, and in 1797 a shilling rate which amounted to £86-18-0d. Two churchwardens, Samuel Nosworthy of Narracombe, and John Rowell of Colesworthy, were elected for an unprecedented period of six years to see the job completed. In 1796 the entries include: 'Drawing up the Agreement and Stamp for Casting the Bells 10/6, Expenses when the Bells were taken down 2/6, postage of 4 letters to Cullompton 1/10, a journey to Cullompton for two men and two horses for two days to see the weight of the bells £1-1-0, paid Mr Bilbie's men for attendance to help weigh the bells 1/-.' From this we know that they were re-cast by the firm of Thomas Bilbie of Cullompton and the total cost was £95-2-6d, paid in three instalments. One of the first times the newly cast bells were rung was on the victory over the Dutch Fleet in 1797 at the Battle of Camperdown.

Ilsington bellringers at Bickington c.1910. Back row l-r: 1. unknown; 2. Bill Redstone; 3. Bill Roberts. Front row l-r: 1. Oliver Roberts; 2. unknown; 3. unknown; 4. Tom Tarr.

CHURCH MUSIC AND CHOIRS

The use of an organ to accompany services is a comparatively modern innovation in rural parish churches, dating from about the middle of the nineteenth century. Traditionally, the accompaniment was by a group of instrumentalists. At Ilsington this consisted of a set of stringed instruments called viols which were the forerunners of today's violin, viola, cello and double-bass. Church records contain details of the costs relating to the church music:

1779 Mending the Base Viol and carriage £1.2.0 Strings for the viols and new bridge for the Counter Viol. A box for the Base Viol.

1780 Mr Bennett for teaching the Singers. £7.4.9

1781 Strings for the Viols 7s.6d.

1782 Strings for the Viols. 6s.6d.

1784 Viol strings omitted last year 2s.5d. Strings for 3 Viols 5s.11½d

1785 Mr Taylor instructing the Singers 10s.6d.

1786 Richard Taylor for instructing the Singers 15s.

1787 The old Singers for repairing the Viols 8.s.2d. Richard Taylor instructing the Singers 1s.3d.

1793 Strings for 4 Viols 11s.6d. Richard Taylor candles for ye Singers 1s.3d.

1794 Richard Taylor for Instructing the Singers and Candles 10s.6d.

Above: *Ilsington church choir 1955, cross bearer Barry Squire. Others include Aubrey Warren, Tom Coventry, Bill Towell, Alan Carpenter, Richard Smith, Gerry Towell, Colin Leggate, and the vicar, Rev. B.R.L. Smith.*

Ilsington church choir 1955.   Back row l-r: 1. Wendy Carpenter (Gibson); 2. Annabel Dixon; 3. Valerie Carpenter (Frost); 4. Nanette Gourd; 5. Helen Leggate.   Front row l-r: 1. Valerie Smith; 2. Janet Carpenter (Perkins) 3. Diana Leggate; 4. Margaret Wills (Klinkenberg); 5. Shirley Squire.

Ilsington church choir, including Edward Knapman, Jonathan Garrish, Peter Leitch, Jonathan Leitch, Alan Wheelhouse, Andrew Cottrell, Jacky Leitch, Marjorie Smith, Debbie Maxwell, Sandra Cornish, Janet Pope, Jackie Wills and the Rev. D.W. Reynolds.

Right: *In 1948 an appeal was made for contributions towards a new burial ground – the cost thought to be £400.*

Below: *The parish bier under restoration. It was originally used by the parishioners in the Liverton and South Knighton area to carry coffins to St Michael's church for burial during the First World War and after. Restoration is being carried out by Geoff Hill and Les Mann.*

New Burial Ground
ILSINGTON

The day is approaching when it will be practically impossible to find burial sites in the present churchyard. The Church Council have therefore decided to purchase a piece of land for a new burial ground, and they are negotiating for a piece, not far from the Church, just over an acre in extent. The cost, including fees and preliminary lay-out, will be about £400. All parishioners, irrespective of creed, will have a right to burial there. We therefore, as representing the Church Council, appeal to all parishioners to subscribe the necessary funds as soon as possible while the land is still available.

We are sending this letter to every house in the parish in the confident hope that each family will make a contribution, large or small. Authorised collectors will call at each house shortly ; or donations may be sent to the Treasurer of the Fund :—

COL. PITMAN,
THE CLEFT,
GREEN LANE,
ILSINGTON.

This concerns the whole parish, so that we trust the whole parish will respond generously.

H. C. COLLINGS, *Vicar.*

J. M. BUCHAN, } *Church-*
C. F. WILLS, } *wardens.*

CHURCH PEOPLE

Left: *The Rev. J.D.H. Patch, vicar of Ilsington 1908–32.*

Below: *Remembrance Sunday, 1963 with the Rev. John Donaldson (vicar), Dick Wills and John Turnbull (churchwardens).*

Above: *Remembrance Sunday, 1993. Churchwardens Dick Wills and Tony Woodason lead the vicar, the Rev. Cliff Curd, and members of the Ilsington and Bickington branch of the Royal British Legion.*

The vicar Rev. Cliff Curd abseils down the church tower to raise money for charity, 1996.

The vicar Rev. John Donaldson and churchwardens Bill Blinston and Dick Wills - said to be the youngest trio ever!

• METHODISM •

In the late 18th and the early part of the 19th century mining and quarrying flourished in the parish. Many families from Cornwall came to work in the district bringing with them non-conformity and adding to the Dissenters already here. At Ilsington in 1821 following the visitation of the parish by Bishop Carey of Exeter he said there were Wesleyans and Baptists in the parish and non-conformist preachers 'frequented this parish weekly.' Jonathan Palk was the vicar and he had a curate at Ilsington. He had been vicar for 35 years and replied that he had a licence for non-residence on account of illness and infirmities.

In 1744 at a visit of Bishop Claggett of Exeter it was said there were no Dissenters. The vicar John Petvin lived at Ashburton and was vicar there and schoolmaster, and his curate at Ilsington was Alexander Laskey.

In 1764 Bishop Keppell of Exeter; visited Ilsington, and found the vicar was Charles Bedford who was also the vicar of Lewannick in Cornwall, where he lived.

In 1830 Oliver Henwood the Wesleyan minister of Ashburton applied for a house in Haytor Vale to be licenced 'as a place of religious worship by an Assembly of Protestants.' By 1840 the Methodist company at the higher end of the parish totalled 8 led by Joseph Taylor and John Sowton who had just come to rent Smallacombe Farm. At Liverton, William Cummings as class leader exercised 'oversight' of 7 members combining this with duties of Society steward and functions of Host at Ilsington where a service was conducted every Sunday evening at 6 o'clock, the preacher having held a service earlier at Liverton.

By 1841 Ilsington had a resident minister, Joseph Kirk, living at Smallacombe who became Society steward for Ilsington. Collections averaged 4 shillings. That year two new chapels were registered at Liverton, one at Rackwoods near Coldeast and the other in Liverton Village. In the next few years, however, Methodism declined in the parish with some members leaving the parish and with 'backsliders,' as they were called, leaving the chapels. In this critical situation the Liverton members transferred to Ilsington.

The Honeywell Weslyan Chapel c.1905. Built in 1852, services before that date were held in the kitchen of Honeywell Farmhouse, home of William Lambshead. Mr and Mrs Basil Philp who now farm at Honeywell say there is still a room called 'the Minister's Room' which the circuit minister used when preaching there.

Ilsington Methodist chapel (left) and Portland Villa built by William Lambshead about 1870 on his retirement from Honeywell Farm.

Portland Villa.

In 1847 William Lambshead aged 22 returned to his native village with his newly-wed wife, to farm at Honeywell where he had been born. In the next 63 years he rendered magnificent service to the community. Now young Mr Lambshead on his return gave wholehearted support to Mr Cummings and began his preaching when one Sunday evening the appointed person did not arrive and he carried on instead. From then on, an additional meeting was held every Sunday afternoon in the farm kitchen. The idea of 'a place of their own' soon arose and Mr Lambshead offered a piece of his land as a gift. No time was wasted and the chapel was opened on 1 January 1852. Within a year the membership had risen from 4 to 40 and the following year the building was enlarged, and soon membership was more than 100. Then came the closure of many mines and quarries, but there was a strong nucleus and numbers were maintained for the next 80 years or so.

Grandchildren of William Cummings, Mrs Alice Heathman and Frederick Cummings, and members of the Lambshead family, must be mentioned, and countless others past and present who have laboured for the Glory of God.

Lambshead was born at Honeywell Farm on 12 August 1825 elder son of William and Mary Lambshead who was formerly Miss Angel of Scorriton. When he was 6 some terrible tragedy struck Honeywell and within 4 months his grandfather William (aged 73) sister Elizabeth (2 years),

Peter Collins all ready for a chapel Sunday School outing.

father William (43 years) and servant Elizabeth Brewer (aged 15) had died. Four years later a relation who had come to farm Honeywill to help the young widow died at 39, and six years later the young Lambshead family were orphaned by the death of their mother. Mary was 17, William 16, Thomas 14 and Sarah 10. William went to live with relatives at Stoke Gabriel and there, under the influence of farm labourer George Callard, attended the local Wesleyan Chapel.

• ILSINGTON CHARITIES •

It was the custom in the 16th and early 17th centuries that when one made a will sums of money were left to the parishes where one lived or held property. Some local examples are :

Thomas Ford of Bagtor left £6 to the poor of Ilsington, to remain in stock for the use of the poor for ever. Walter Leare of the Barbados who owned lands in Ilsington, left the poor of Ilsington £5. Richard Leare to the poor of Ilsington twenty shillings.

These bequests and many others were used mainly for buying land for posterity and so Ilsington Parish Lands Charity came into being.

Through the centuries the profits of these lands have been used for providing for the poor of the parish, especially after the passing of the Poor Law of Elizabeth I where, with decay of the manorial jurisdiction, the parish was given the legal responsibilities of looking after and housing the parish poor. The charity was divided into two parts one for the relief of the poor who were sick, aged, disabled and unable to work, and the other for housing. The Church House at Ilsington became the Poor House, and later a cottage was built on some waste land beside the road near Smokey Cross on the road towards Haytor.

The charity still exists today and distributes help to parishioners in times of need, and with electricity bills and parcels at Christmas time.

Smokey Cottage, near Smokey Cross, was originally built in 1819 as an extension to the parish Poor House in Ilsington village by the Overseers of the Poor. It was built on a strip of waste land (consequently the site is very narrow) and was sold after 1836 (when the parish poor came into the care of the Guardians of the Newton Abbot Union), then becoming three cottages

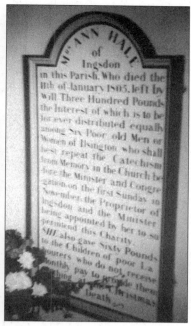

St Michael's Cottages at Ilsington, formerly the Church House, and from the 17th century, the parish Poor House, where the very poor and their families were housed and looked after on the parish Poor Rates. Above right: Ann Hale's memorial in Ilsington church.

Candy's Charity

Legend has it that William Candy, a travelling musician in the late 17th century, gathered enough money to buy a farm, and when he died he bequeathed it to the kind of people who enabled him to buy it – the generous poor! Whether this is true or not, I do not know, but it is a fact that he was a native of Dorset and purchased a farm at Halford in Ilsington parish known as Hore's Tenement in 1713. By his will in 1727 after some small bequests to members of his family he left the farm to the vicar and churchwardens of Ilsington, that they should let the farm and dispose of its profits for ever to provide:

To 9 poor men of Ilsington parish, of sober life and who attend the parish church every Sunday, a new hat, coat, shirt and a pair of shoes. Also to those 9 men, the sum of 9 shillings should be spent in giving them food and drink on Christmas Day, and that the Vicar should have a £1 for preaching a funeral sermon yearly on the day of Candy's death.

Through the years it has become necessary that these details be revised and now coats are only given to parishioners who apply, preference being given to outdoor workers, and the charity is used to assist the other charities in providing parcels to the aged at Christmas time. The applicants for the so-called Candy Coats have decreased latterly, some fifty years ago there were about forty annually, and Ilsington people became known as 'Greybacks' as they wore the same type of coats!

Anne Hale

Mrs Ann Hale (née Carpenter) widow of Charles Hale of Ingsdon Manor, by her will dated 1804, left £300:

to be invested and the interest to be paid yearly in providing clothing for the children of the poorest labourers, and to six of the oldest poor men or women of the parish who could repeat the catechism perfectly in Ilsington Church on the first Sunday in November, the sum of...

However by the failure of an Ashburton bank most of this money was lost within a few years, and was eventually repaid by the then vicar of Ilsington, the Rev. Jonathan Palk.

In 1823 it is said that the contest among the old people best able to say their catechism publicly in church was very fierce. The names given in one of the old record books of the successful candidates were Michael Cumming (77), Richard

An account from Ilsington School Charity in 1874 listing the names of children whose fees had been met for for one quarter year.

Penny (77), Mary May (77), Gertrude Honeywill (76), Susanna Colman (75), and Susanna Layman (73), with no less than nine others being unsuccessful! No wonder that a hundred years later the Rev. J.D.H. Patch stopped the spectacle being held during the church service, 'for he said there was much heckling and prompting from the congregation and it was more like an entertainment than a service in church.'

Jane Ford

Jane Ford, spinster, the daughter of Thomas Ford of Bagtor Manor, and sister of the dramatist John Ford, by her will dated 1663 bequeathed lands in Ashburton, part of her Manor of Halwell, upon trust the rents and profits to be used for ever, to pay for the schooling and books for poor children of the parish of Ilsington, until they could read the Holy Bible.

Since then these instructions have been altered to suit the times, especially with the introduction of free schooling in the 19th century. At one time children received sums of money yearly for their attendance, conduct and progress at school, the money being banked for them and paid when they finally left. Now part of it is allocated annually to children at the two primary schools, Ilsington and Blackpool, on an equal basis, and is paid to them when they leave primary school. The surplus is given to the schools for books.

Many thousands of Ilsington children have benefited from this charity since 1664, and many have learnt to read and write who otherwise would have been illiterate.

Widger's Charity

William Furneaux Widger of Sigford House by his will dated 1888 left £300 to Ilsington parish for the annual distribution of blankets and coals amongst the deserving poor at Christmas time. This has been used by the trustees of this charity in providing blankets and coals and occasionally lengths of serge. In selecting the recipients consideration was given to persons with large families, or who were old and incapacitated from work.

Today the original £300 does not provide much annual income, and not many blankets are able to be given. Also people do not want blankets these days and ask for duvets instead!

3 - Schools

Small dame schools existed from early times in Ilsington parish, greatly helped by Miss Jane Ford and her charity. The story of the collapse of one of these schools is told in the previous chapter. Fortunately all survived though 'some were cut and bruised, to remind them of the danger they were in. One sweet boy named Humphry Degon, was missing, but when rubble was moved, he rose up and ran away home, none the worse for his adventure.'

In the 19th century church schools were built at Ilsington and Blackpool in the lower end of the parish, and both still exist, although the Blackpool school has been greatly enlarged and now caters for 270 children.

INGSDON CONVENT

Ingsdon Manor was purchased by the White Sisters from St Brieuc in Brittany in 1902 who opened St Michael's Convent there. It became a very popular school between the two World Wars. Unfortunately it had to close down in 1972 through a shortage of nuns in teaching orders. Then it became a school for backward boys, but it was entirely destroyed by fire and was demolished and replaced by some large modern residences.

There follow many photographs associated with the schools, the teachers, and the schoolchildren of Ilsington over the years.

19TH CENTURY SCHOOLS

One of the earliest known pictures of schoolchildren in Ilsington, taken before 1883 when John Heathman became headteacher, possibly during Miss Allen's time.

19TH CENTURY SCHOOLS

This photograph belonged to Mr and Mrs Frank Berry of Lounston. It was taken when John Heathman was headteacher in 1883. Possibly John Clarke (second from left, front row) and Pharoah Grose (next on right) appear.

Apparently John Heathman as a young man shortly after his appointment in 1883, with his wife as assistant, and a young Jessie Clark. One of the younger boys is possibly the author's father, Sydney Wills, who went to school at Ilsington in the 1880s.

Ilsington Church School with headteacher John Heathman and assistant Jessie Clark, 1890s. The woman in the mortar board is Ruth Tarr (Sanders).

19TH CENTURY SCHOOLS

Above and below: *Blackpool school 16 March 1899. The headteacher is Emma Snow, the teacher Miss Beavis, and monitor Eva Yelland.*

Below left: *A solid silver token given to all children of Ilsington parish. It is inscribed 'Souvenir of Mr and Mrs John Warren's return from Australia after 37 years absence 1863–1900.' The couple went to live at Silverbrook Mine Cottage.*

Above: *Blackpool School 1899.*

Blackpool School c.1910.

SCHOOLS 1900–1950

Blackpool School, 1919. Back row: 1. Jack Richards, 2. Bill Saunders, 3. Tom Frost, 4. Bill Muggeridge, 5. Eli Lang, 6. Joe Lang, 7. Harold Manley, 8. Reg Manley, 9. George Frost, 10. Mr Flower. Second row: 1. Jack Bond, 2. Harold Osborne, 3. Sam Wrayford, 4. Les Manley, 5. Bert Black, 6. Reg Cox, 7. Tom Squire. Sitting: 1. John Billinghurst, 2. William Becksmith, 3. Tom Lang, 4. Bill Rowe, 5. Chris Squire, 6. Tony Satterley, 7. Sid Lang, 8. Edward Cleave, 9. Bill Rowell. Front row: 1. Sid Brock, 2. Jim Gulley, 3. Bill Avery, 4. Jack Penellum.

Ilsington Primary School, c.1928. Back row: 2. Bill Giles, 3. Harry Heathman, 6. George Northway. Middle row: 1. Joyce Heathman, 2. Joan Carpenter, 3. Lily Collins, 6. Edna Giles. Front row: 1. Lewis Roberts, 3. Lily Northway, 4. Betty Derges, 5. Marjorie Smerdon, 7. Gwen Harvey, 8. Vi French, 9. Lawrence Cornish, 10. Alfred Smerdon.

Blackpool Primary School, c.1928. Back row: 1. Miss Slee, 2. Jim Eveleigh, 3. Cyril, Lang, 4. Sid Cox, 5. Roy Blackler, 6. Percy Lang, 7. Charles Gulley. Middle row: 1. Lily Sampson, 2. Audrey Burrows, 3. Ruby Penellum, 4. Daisy Brock, 5. Irene Penellum, 6. Tilly Squire, 7. Mary Manley. Front row: 1. Joyce Smith, 2. Ivy Parsons, 3. Norah Collins, 4. Dinkie Alford.

SCHOOLS 1900–1950

Blackpool School, 1920s. Back row:
1. Sam Cox, 2. Cyril Lang, 3. Reg Rowe,
4. Jim Saunders, 5. Bill Avery, 6. Walter
Sampson, 7. Percy Lang, 8. Roy Blackler.
Standing: 1. Ivor Guest, 2. Joyce Smith,
3. Norah Collins, 4. Audrey Burrows,
5. Tilly Squire, 6. Joan Watts, 7. Phyllis
Burrows, 8. Mary Manley, 9. Irene
Penellum, 10. Ruby Penellum. Sitting:
1. Alice Frost, 2. Gladys Alford, 3. Lily
Sampson 4. Doris Collins. Standing
on right: 1. Rex Moyle, 2. Brenda
Rowe. Front row: 1. Cyril Warren,
2. George Cleave, 3. Ernie Brock; 4. Reg
England, 5. Bill Burrows, 6. Walter
Squire.

Blackpool School, 1920s. The pho-
tograph is known to have been
taken after November 1919 since
that was when children from
Chipley and South Knighton came
to Blackpool, and some of those
children are in this group. Back
row: 1. Tom Howard, 2. Tom
Squire, 3. Eli Lang, 4. Maurice
Spratt, 5. Lottie Howard, 6. Eva
Spratt. Standing: 1. Winnie
Brock, 2. Tom Lang, 3. Doris
Davis, 4. Bill Rowell, 5. Bill Davis,
6. Joe Lang, 7. Jack Penellum, 8.
Violet Rowell, 9. Doris Penellum.
Sitting: 1. Dorothy Brock, 2. Kitty
Squire, 3. Tilly Squire, 4. Flo

Squire, 5. Percy Lang, 6. Reg Eveleigh. Front row: 1. Lewis Penellum, 2. Tom Penellum, 3. Maurice
Towell, 4. Bill Towell, 5. Annie Lang, 6. Rene Penellum, 7. Cyril Lang, 8. Sid Lang.

Blackpool School, 1920s. Back
row: 1. Jim Eveleigh, 2. Sid Cox,
3. Tom Penellum, 4. Jim
Saunders, 5. Hugh Johns, 6. Tom
Frost, 7. Fred Howe, 8. unknown.
Middle row: 1. Roy Blackler, 2.
Bill Towell, 3. Nellie Eveleigh, 4.
Ivy Parsons, 5. Annie Lang, 6.
Phyllis Burrows, 7. Rene
Penellum, 8. Audrey Burrows, 9.
Bill Avery, 10. unknown. Front
row: 1. Walter Sampson, 2. Tilly
Squire, 3. Mary Manley, 4. Miss
Proudlock, 5. Daisy French, 6.
Nora Collins, 7. Reg Rowe.

SCHOOLS 1900–1950

*Blackpool School, 1920s.
Back row: 2. Eveleigh,
3. Howard, 5. Percy Lang,
6. Howard, 8. Miss Lee.
Middle row: 1. Jack
Penellum, 2. Ivy Parsons,
3. Joyce Smith, 4. Alice Frost,
5. Doris Collins, 6. Gladys
Alford, 7. Ruby Penellum,
8. Lily Sampson, 9. George
Cleave. Girls sitting:
1. Winnie Tolley, 2. Brenda
Rowe, 3. Amy Sampson.
Front row: 1. Reg Burrows,
2. Rex Moyle, 3. Bill Guest,
4. Cyril Warren.*

*Blackpool School, 1920s. Back row: 1. Miss Slee 2. Reg Harris, 3. Norman Tolley, 4. Bill Guest, 5. Reg
Burrows, 6. Aubrey Warren, 7. Edward Tolley, 8. Ron Squire, 9. Fred Sampson, 10. Fred Alford. Middle
row: 3. Norman Penellum, 4. Dorothy Burgess, 5. Marjorie Alford, 6. Mary Lang, 7. Phyllis Frost,
10. Dorothy Worth, 11. Gordon Howard, 12. Cyril Greenway. Front row: 1. Fred Cox, 2. Derek Towell,
4. Cecily Archer, 5. Betty Sampson, 6. Ken Towell, 7. Alan Cleave.*

*Blackpool School, 1920s. Back row: 1. Sid Wilson
2. Cyril Greenway, 3. Reg Burrows, 5. Bill Guest,
6. Fred Wilson, 7. Harry Howard. Middle row:
1. Ron Squire, 2. Alan Cleave, 3. Fred Saunders,
4. Nellie Guest, 5. Amy Sampson, 6. Marjorie
?; 7. Dorothy Worth, 8. Norman Penellum,
9. Gordon Howard. Girls Seated: 1. Mary
Lang, 2. Phyllis Frost, 3. Delcie Towell, 4. ?;
Front row: 1. Reg Harris, 2. Walter Squire,
4. Edward Tolley, 5. Percy Lang.*

SCHOOLS 1900–1950

Blackpool School 1930s. Back row: *1. Rene Selley; 2. Evelyn England, 3. Miss Slee, 4. Cyril Greenway, 5. Bill Guest, 6. Fred Wilson, 7. Reg Burrows, 8. Aubrey Warren, 9. Harry Howard, 10. Miss Marion Sanders. Middle row: 1. George Cleave, 2. Fred Saunders, 3. Norman Tolley, 4. Phyllis Frost, 5. Mary Lang, 6. Nellie Guest, 7. Edward Tolley, 8. Gordon Howard, 9. Norman Penellum, 10. Amy Sampson, 11. Ron Squire. Front row: 1. Betty Sampson, 2. Betty Watts, 3. Cecily Archer, 4. Dorothy Worth.*

Ilsington School 1930s. Back row: *1. Bill Giles; 2. Norman Cornish, 3. George Derges, 4. Bill Derges, 5. Alf Morrish, 6. Lewis Giles, 7. John Nunn, 8. Bill Dymond. Second row: 1. Margaret Tarr, 2. Florrie Cornish, 3. Dora Dymond, 4. Lily Northway, 5. Betty Derges, 6. Helena Back, 7. Marjorie Smerdon, 8. Margaret Giles, 9. Nora Carpenter, 10. Winnie Morley, 11. Winnie Tarr, 12. Emily Northway, 13. Ken Nunn, 14. Miss Napper. Third row: 1. Miss Iles, 2. Tom Kinsman, 3. Joan Carpenter, 4. Edna Giles, 5. Rene Harvey, 6. Lily Collins, 7. Pat Flay, 8. Joyce Heathman, 9. Gwen Harvey, 10. Doreen Head, 11. Cathie Brewer, 12. Annie Willcocks, 13. Hilda Honeywill, 14. Joyce Retallick 15. Peggy Dart, 16. Fred Dymond. Front row: 1. Dick Kinsman, 2. Rosemary Back, 3. Doreen Brewer, 4. George Northway, 5. Alfred Smerdon, 6. Lewis Roberts, 7. Dick Wills, 8. Fred Honeywill, 9. Lawrence Cornish, 10. George Roberts, 11. Raymond Smerdon, 12. David Crosby, 13. Desmond Roberts.*

SCHOOLS 1900–1950

Ilsington School 1930s. Back row: *1. Winnie Morley, 2. Winnie Tarr, 3. Betty Derges, 4. Nora Carpenter, 5. Kathie Brewer, 6. Annie Willcocks, 7. Helena Back, 8. Joyce Heathman. 9. Lily Northway, 10. Doreen Head.* Second row: *1. Miss Iles, 2. Gwen Harvey, 3. Rene Retallick, 4. Rene Harvey, 5. Pat Flay, 6. Rosemary Back, 7. Joan Carpenter, 8. Edna Giles, 9. Hilda Roberts, 10. Doreen Brewer, 11. Doris Morley, 12. Margaret Giles, 13. Miss Napper.* Kneeling: *1. Dick Wills, 2. Bill Dymond, 3. Lawrence Cornish, 4. Peggy Dart, 5. Ivy Wallen, 6. Doris Back, 7. Leslie Bradford, 8. George Northway.* Sitting: *1. Dick Cornish, 2. Alf Harvey, 3. Gilbert Roberts, 4. Bob Flay, 5. Fred Dymond.*

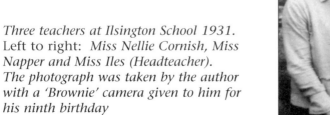

Three teachers at Ilsington School 1931. Left to right: Miss Nellie Cornish, Miss Napper and Miss Iles (Headteacher). The photograph was taken by the author with a 'Brownie' camera given to him for his ninth birthday

SCHOOLS 1900–1950

Ilsington schoolboys, 1930. Left to right: *Raymond Smerdon, unknown, unknown, Bill Derges, George Derges, Will Giles (spindle); Lewis Giles, Alfred Smerdon, Dick Wills, John MacKinley, David Crosby.*

Ilsington School 1930s. Back row: *1. Winnie Morley, 2. Betty Derges, 3. Nora Carpenter, 4. Edna Giles, 5. Joyce Heathman, 6. Lily Harvey.* Second row: *1. Lily Collins, 2. Pat Flay, 3. Peggy Dart, 4. Doreen Brewer, 5. Joan Carpenter, 6. Joyce Retallick.* Third row: *1. Gwen Harvey, 2. George Northway. 3. Winnie Tarr, 4. Hilda Roberts, 5. Rene Harvey, 6. Cathie Brewer, 7. Doris Morley, 8. Dick Wills, 9. Doreen Head, 10. Annie Willcocks, 11, Laurence Cornish.* Fourth row: *1. Miss May Iles (Headteacher), 2. Peter Harvey. 3. Fred Dymond, 4. Lewis Roberts, 5. Leslie Bradford, 6. Alf Harvey, 7. Dick Cornish, 8. Desmond Roberts, 9. Miss Napper.* Front row: *1. Bob Flay, 2. Dorothy Honeywill. 3. Pearl Mortimore, 4. Peter Collins, 5. Gilbert (Sam) Roberts.*

Blackpool schoolboys and girls on a bike ride. Left to right: *Reg Harris, Fred Saunders, Fred Wilson, Norman Penellum, Gordon Howard, Fred Alford, Betty Sampson, unknown, unknown.*

Blackpool School 1950. Back row: *1. Jean Snell 2. Rachel Cousins, 3. Vivien Leigh, 4. unknown, 5. Rosemary Brown, 6. unknown, 7. Kathleen Lang, 8. Violet Lees, 9. Shirley Sampson.* Second row: *1. Barry Caunter, 2. Michael Whiting, 3. Michael Pady, 4. Colin Black, 5. D. Thorne, 6. Eric Hingston, 7. Derek Bourne, 8. David Lang, 9. Edward Waldron, 10. David Billinghurst, 11. Keith Penellum, 12. Keith Collins.* Front: *1. ? Cousins, 2. Bernard Saunders, 3. Robert Ralph, 4. Cresswell Waldron, 5. Pat Pady, 6. Cherry Whiting, 7. Sheila Lang, 8. George Miller, 9. Malcolm Miller, 10. Richard Cousins, 11. Christopher Moyle.*

LATER SCHOOLDAYS

Blackpool School 1950. Back row: *1. unknown 2. Jean Snell, 3. Shirley Sampson, 4. Edward Waldron, 5. David Lang, 6. Vivien Leigh, 7. Pamela Billinghurst, 8. Kathleen Lang, 9. Alfred Dibble, 10. Brian Snell, 11. Colin Black, 12. Roy Snell, 13. Michael Whiting.* Second row: *1. Eric Hingston, 2. Michael Pady, 3. Derek Bourne, 4. Diane Sergeant, 5. Valerie Black, 6. Rachael Saunders, 7. Rosemary Brown, 8. Shirley Squire, 9. Violet Lee, 10. Bridget Saunders, 11. Rachel Cousins* Front: *1. Cherry Whiting, 2. Carole Dibble, 3. Carol Foxworthy, 4. Sylvia Foxworthy, 5. Cresswell Waldron, 6. Keith Penellum, 7. Barry Caunter, 8. David Billinghurst, 9. Wendy Snell, 10. Michael Snell, 11. John Small.*

*Blackpool School 1950s.
Back row: 1. Vivien Leigh, 2. Violet Lee, 3. Rosemary Brown, 4. Rachel Cousins, 5. Kathleen Lang. Middle row: 1. Keith Collins, 2. Eric Hingston, 3. unknown, 4. Colin Black, 5. Jean Snell, 6. Diane Sergeant, 7. Shirley Sampson, 8. Sheila Lang, 9. unknown, 10. Colin Wakeham, 11. Derek Bourne, 12. Edward Waldron, 13. unknown.*

Kneeling: *1. David Billinghurst, 2. unknown, 3. Keith Penellum, 4 and 5 unknown, 6. Cherry Whiting, 7. unknown, 8. Bernard Saunders, 9. Michael Whiting, 10 and 11 unknown.* Front: *all unknown except 2. Michael Snell, 7. Barry Snell and 10. Cresswell Waldron.*

LATER SCHOOLDAYS

Blackpool Juniors 1961. Back row: 1. Roger Vooght, 2. Ian Nichols, 3. David Blinston, 4. Martyn Bourne, 5. Trevor Birch, 6. Nigel Johnson, 7. Barry Snell, 8. Mr W. Blinston. Second row: 1. Andrew Hammet, 2. Richard Arthurs, 3. Denise Bray, 4. Janet Andrews, 5. Ann Rosser, 6. Russell Clarke, 7. Paul Newman. Front: 1. Denise Moyle, 2. Christine Vooght, 3. Pauline Penellum, 4. Susan Batey, 5. Jennifer Penellum, 6. Kathleen Morrison.

Blackpool School 1965. Back row: 1. Mr W. Blinston 2. Norman Irish, 3. Sheila Stringfellow, 4. Philip Bourne, 5. Carol Donaldson, 6. unknown, 7. Lindsay Towell, 8. Tommy Vallance. Second row: 1. Moira Nichols, 2. Tony Laskey, 3. ? Clarke, 4. Andrew Towell, 5. Philip Rice, 6. Andrew Hammett, 7. Tina Moyle, 8. Candy Norman, 9. Christine Brinham. Front: 1. Nicola Wrayford, 2. Yvonne Donaldson, 3. Jackie Nichols, 4. David Hammet, 5. Kenny Brinham, 6. unknown, 7. David Armstrong, 8. Beverley Miners, 9. Christine Cove, 10. Barbara Snell.

Blackpool School, C. Colwill with school leavers, 1966. Included are Philip Bourne, K. Brimham, Lindsay Towell, Carol Donaldson, J. Nichols, Beverly Miners and Christine Cove.

LATER SCHOOLDAYS

Blackpool School leavers, 1967 with Rev. J.C. Donaldson, vicar of Ilsington. Standing: 1. Christine Cove, 2. Yvonne Donaldson, 3. Nicola Wrayford, 4. Mary Donaldson, 5. David Armstrong, 6. Tommy Vallance, 7. Brian Edwards, 8. David Hammett. Kneeling: 1. Caroline Twose, 2. Brian Hall.

Blackpool School, 1968. Mrs Josephine George and the Infants class. Back row: 1. Stephen Pascoe, 2. Colin Buckpit, 3. Robert Armstrong, 4. Annette Miners, 5. Adam Poulson, 6. Ann Daniel. Second row: 1. Martin Alford, 2. Ann Rooke, 3. David Elliott, 4. Philip Hornby, 5. Colin Wrayford, 6. Renny Broadway, 7. Lesley Bradford, 8. Lesley Pike. Third row: 1. Roger Cornish, 2. Earl Bradford, 3. Mandy Whiteley, 4. Julie Moss, 5. Tony Calverley, 6. Susan Armstrong, 7. Jeanette Hall. Front: 1. Joanna Latimer, 2. Tina Bray, 3. Shirley Carrett, 4. Linda Snell, 5. Joanna Whiteley, 6. Joanne Palmer, 7. Carolyn Ellis.

Blackpool School mid 1960s. Mrs Josephine George and her class. Back row: 1. unknown, 2. unknown, 3. Andrew Harrison, 4. Neil Harvey, 5. Nathan Hale, 6. Matthew Bearne, 7. Mrs George. Second row: 1. Jeremy McKinley, 2. Adam Cornish, 3. unknown, 4. Jason Bligh, 5. Kate Rampton, 6. Anna Ford, 7. Dean Courtier, 8. unknown. Front: 1. Gary Pearce, 2. Lyndon Townson, 3. Simon Roose, 4. Robin Walker, 5. James Gregory, 6. Joanne Wills, 7. Virginia Denham.

LATER SCHOOLDAYS

Blackpool Juniors with Mrs M. Causey. Back row: 1. Jason Bligh, 2. Adam Cornish, 3. Elizabeth Tilley, 4. Robert Hottot, 5. Nathan Hale, 6. unknown, 7. Anna Ford, 8. Becky Warner, 9. Matthew Bearne, 10. unknown. Second row: 1. Karen Warren, 2. Lisa Jameson, 3. Andrew Harrison, 4. Peter McCauley, 5. Jeffry Choat, 6. Annette Parnell, 7. Neil Harvey, 8. unknown, 9. Joanna Atkinson, 10. Peter Atkinson, 11, Giles Ashman, 12. Sarah Hottot, 13. Jeremy McKinley. Front: 1. Gary Pearce, 2. Geoffrey Mann, 3. Joanna Wills, 4. unknown, 5. Simon Roose, 6–8. unknown, 9. Lyndon Townson, 10. James Gregory.

Ilsington School visit to Exeter Maritime Museum, June 1978. Pictured, left to right , Dominic Towell, Eddie Williams, Stuart Upham, Russell Retallick, Tracey Mann, Janet Pope, Ellis Wills.

Blackpool Juniors with Mrs D. Perkins. Back row: 1. Lisa Jameson, 2. Penny Smith, 3. Sally Hands, 4. Alison Frost, 5. Jeremy Christophers, 6. David Mann, 7. Keith Ellis, 8. Peter Thomas, 9 and 10, unknown. Second row: 1. Sylvia Luscombe, 2. Michael Cannon, 3. Nicola Denham, 4. unknown, 5. Jane Talbot, 6. Shirley McCauley, 7. Terry Parnell, 8. Lorraine Andrews, 9. Nicola Hornby, 10. Esther Famiyeh, 11, unknown. Front: 1. Sarah Clarke, 2. Robert Hottot, 3. Karen Warren, 4. Jenny Heath, 5. Tim Warner, 6. Joan Hands, 7. Jane Prowse, 8. Andrea Harvey, 9. Joan Sanders, 10. William Clarke.

LATER SCHOOLDAYS

Ilsington Primary School 1986. Back row l-r: *1. Philip Pascoe, 2. Gulliver Thoday 3. Fay McCluskey.* Second row: *1. Andrew Gayton, 2. Claire Retallick, 3. Danny ?, 4. Daniel Foster, 5. Donald Gayton, 6. Edric Waghorn.* Third row: *1. Joseph Bosence, 2. Rohan Davidson, 3. Mr Williams (Temporary Headteacher), 4. Kate McCluskey, 5. Mrs Perkins (Infants Teacher), 6. Elliott Retallick, 7. Ross Edwards.* Front row: *1. Kate Bainbridge, 2. Kate Wills, 3. Gemma Aucock.*

Right: *Ilsington School, 1991.* Back Row: *1. Nicola O'Gara, 2. Charles Brassley, 3. Jonathan May, 4. Georgie Wills, 5. James Martin, 6. Matthew Hope, 7. Adam Campkin, 8. Tina May.* Second Row: *1. Tom White, 2. Robert Portus, 3. Claire Marrinan, 4. Claire Bardell, 5. Jeffrey Bardell, 6. Edward Bainbridge, 7. Chris Honeywill, 8. Glen Furze, 9. Ben Downton, 10. Jo Portus, 11. Lee Cooper.* Middle Row: *1. Matthew Lovejoy, 2. Chloe Wills, 3. Tom Bosence, 4. Charlotte Rowe, 5. Alison Rowe, 6. Jan Bosence, 7. Russell Bowden, 8. Erin Sheldon, 9. Samantha May, 10. Briony Davidson, 11. Megan Jones, 12. Caroline Brassley.* Seated: *1. Georgia Day, 2. Evan Marrinan, 3. Kandi Smith, 4. Michael Lavers, 5. Carol Mantell (Headteacher), 6. Chris Campkin, 7. Julienne Kingsley (Assistant Teacher), 8. Amy Sullivan, 9. Cathy Downton (Music Teacher), 10. Jenna Roberts, 11. Simon McCredie.* Front Row: *1. Michelle Head, 2. Laura Lavers, 3. Rosa Petherick, 4. Michael Tapp, 5. Gemma Nicholls.*

Ilsington School, 1991. Back Row: *1. Laura Lavers, 2. Gemma Nicholls, 3. Nicholas Tiley, 4. Chloe Wills, 5. Tom Bosence, 6. Nicholas Astbury, 7. Josh Widdecombe, 8. Christopher Campkin, 9. Evan Marrinan, 10. Georgia Day.* Fourth row: *1. Michael Tapp, 2. Michael Lavers, 3. Adam Campkin, 4. Megan Jones, 5. Joanna Portus, 6. Jenna Waghorn, 7. Claire Marrinan, 8. Ben Downton, 9 Amy Sullivan, 10. Michelle Head, 11. Kayleigh O'Gara.* Third Row: *1. Rosa Petherick 2. Evie Bowden, 3. Jenna Roberts, 4. Nicola O'Gara, 5. Robert Portus, 6. Claire Bardell, 7. Georgie Wills, 8. Briony Davidson, 9. Stephanie Tiley, 10. Thomas White, 11. Alana Waghorn, 12. Michael Sheppherd.* Second Row: *1. Simon Roberts, 2. Hannah Bosence, 3. James Guppy, 4. Mrs Moore, 5. Matthew Pilkington, 6. Mrs Mantell (Headteacher), 7. Lee Cooper, 8. Mrs Downton, 9. Claire Jones, 10. Jonathan Walker, 11. Robert Tapp.* Front Row: *1. Russell White, 2. Natalie Petherick, 3. unknown, 4. Ben Mansfield, 5. Luke Sullivan, 6. Richard Nicholls, 7. Rebecca Head, 8. Helen Cawthraw, 9. Catherine Blackwell.*

4 - Sports and Entertainments

This chapter touches on just a few of the activities and events that have entertained parishioners over the years.

COCK FIGHTING

Squire Woodley of Halshanger was very fond of cock-fighting. He kept a lot of game-cocks, trained for the job, with combs cut tight to their heads. Jack Corrick could recall a meeting at Silverbrook Mines. We boys got to know of it and hid behind the bushes. People brought their game-cocks in hampers, and they all started to crow. The crowd broke up in disorder when some policemen appeared on the scene.

HARE HUNTING

Jack Corrick goes on to say, 'Tom Hamble hunted the Chudleigh Harriers and now and again they would meet at the Rock Inn, Haytor Vale. They would come to Smallacombe to draw. Farmer Bob Foale was there then. My father was horseman and Farmer Bob would tell him to find a hare, most times in the hedge above Oldertown. I can recall one night when father and I were in the stable doing them up for the night, the harriers were out in the meadow in full cry. In the bright moon-light.'

ILSINGTON CRICKET CLUB

Cricket was played at Ilsington way back in the 1860s organised by my grandfather and his brothers, for it is said that Curate Edwards of that day could throw a cricket ball across the valley from Narracombe fields to the Sanctuary fields. But it was in 1894 that the first Ilsington Cricket Club was formed when Herbert Lyon, son of the diarist Alfred Lyon of Middlecott became its first captain.

Ilsington Wanderers Cricket Club c.1909. Back row: *Herbert Harris, Tom Ball, Ronald Harris, Ike Sanders, Sydney Grose, unknown.* Middle row: *E. Terrell, Sydney Wills, Harry Harris (Capt), W. Roberts, J. Webb.* Front: *Charlie (C.H.B. Wills), Norman Grose.*

Charlie Wills (1912-1954) practising cricket on the 'Blacksmith's Shop' ground in the meadow at Narracombe.

Cricket tea being taken at Narracombe c.1928. Teas were always provided to all the cricketers playing (and spectators if they paid), at 5.00pm. The author's mother and Mrs Grose provided the tea, always 'Ashburton' buns with cream and jam, a fruit slab cake and cups of tea. Appearing in the photo is the author, the author's mother, Mrs Grose, Bill Cator and Jack Brewer.

For the first few years matches were played in 'Jubilee Field' in Ilsington village, where South Park now stands. Then the pitch was moved to Cross Parks on the Sigford road. There are unfortunately no records of those early years, only the names of the officials which included Herbert Lyon, John Aplin, Harry Harris, the Rev. Williamson (vicar of Bickington), John Honeywill and Sydney Wills.

In 1902 a second team called the Ilsington Wanderers was formed. Their pitch was at Narracombe, and from then until its final match at the end of 1947 there are records in existence of virtually every ball bowled. During those years the names of Ilsington and cricket, and I may add, that of my father Sydney Wills, became synonymous: regularly every Saturday afternoon during the summer months everything stopped for cricket, including farming, and it was the chief topic of conversation for the remainder of the week.

The game filled a big social gap, from the time when the 5½ day week came into being, until the more affluent post Second World War days. Teams came from all over South Devon to play and return matches were arranged, first travelling on bicycles and horses, and then by charabanc motor coaches. Annual fixtures were played between Ilsington and Shobrooke, a village near Crediton, on Whit Mondays and August Bank Holidays, and also at the Royal Naval College, Dartmouth. Several keen supporters travelled with the Ilsington team on these occasions, and the home team eagerly awaited to see who the visitors had brought with them. A keen band of the Ilsington cricketers' wives supplied the tea at Narracombe under the poplar trees; it always consisted of splits, which were called 'Ashburtons' in those days, liberally spread with thick clotted cream and strawberry jam. And it never rained! (Or did it?)

Although the pitch at Narracombe was not very level and the outfield was usually long grass, Ilsington produced some good cricketers. In 1937 my older brother Charlie Wills, a devout cricketer, persuaded me to help him produce a *Wisden* of Ilsington cricket. We went through all the old

Ilsington Cricket team off to Dartmouth, 1924, with Bill Flay (trilby hat), Fred Derges, and Sydney Wills (in front on right).

Ilsington Wanderers Cricket Club c.1911. Back row: *Tom Ball; J. Webb, Herbert Harris, Reggie Harvey, unknown, Ronald Harris. Sitting: Charlie (C.H.B.) Wills, unknown, Sydney Wills, Harry Harris (Capt), unknown, the Rev. J.D.H. Patch. Front row: the Donaldson brothers.*

Ilsington Cricket Club 1938. Back row: *Bill Gill, Charlie Wills, Sydney Wills, Bill Heathman, Bill Flay.* Second row: *Hawkins (umpire), Sidney Grose (in cap), Lewis Giles, Charlie Heathman, Lawrence Cornish, Arthur Courtier.* Front: *Vernon Brewer and Dick Wills (scorer).*

Ilsington Cricket Club, 1938, in Narracombe Meadow. Back row: *Lewis Giles, Charlie Wills, Bill Flay, Sydney Wills, Lawrence Cornish, Sidney Grose, Arthur Courtier, Bill Heathman, Bill Gill.* Front row: *Dick Wills, Vernon Brewer and Charlie Heathman.*

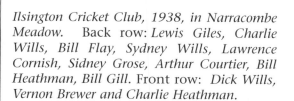

Ilsington Cricket Club, 1929. Back row: *George Brimblecombe, Bill Flay, Len Harris.* Middle row: *Bill Brimblecombe, George Rowe, Sydney Wills (Capt), Sidney Grose, Bill Gill.* Front row: *Bill Cator, Jack Brewer and Norman Lampard.*

Ilsington Cricket Team c.1975. Back row l-r: *1. Alan Jones, 2. Dave Wills, 3. Brian Roberts, 4. Phil Rice, 5. Ron Westaway, 6. Barry Squire.* Front row: *Derek White, 2. Ray Bartlett, 3. Roger Carpenter, 4. Rob Wills, 5. Richard Maxwell.*

score books, extracted the averages for every year and all sorts of records such as fifty or more runs in an innings, record partnerships, highest and lowest aggregates, notable bowling feats, highest number of wickets in a season, etc. Thus it is known that Edwin Molyneux took all 10 wickets in a match against Denbury in 1900, and that my father Sydney Wills took 9 wickets for 11 runs (and he caught the 10th man) in a match versus Highweek in 1904, and that Les Heathman took 9 wickets for 41 runs at R.N.C. Dartmouth in 1947. In 1908 Ern Terrell made a record total of 398 runs in a season, followed by Captain Harry Harris' 375 in 1906 and Bill Flay's 352 in 1926. The highest individual score to be made at home was 102 not out by C. Phillips versus Bickington in 1900, but scores of 156 made by my brother Charlie Wills v R.N.C. Dartmouth in 1937, 133 by V.R. Bennett v Totnes in 1908, 115 by W.S. Dobson v Exminster in 1909, and 82 by Bill Flay v Haytor Vale (Liverton) in 1926 were made away.

Many names are recorded of people playing for Ilsington, in fact there were very few residents of those years who were not roped in to fill a gap at some time or another. On one occasion, I remember, a regular player for Ilsington was actually kidnapped on the road when he was on his way to play for another team!

Perhaps a little of the feeling for cricket in those days can be recaptured by the following verse from my father's newspaper cutting book :-

There's a breathless hush in the close tonight
Ten to make and the match to win,
A bumping pitch and a blinding light,
An hour to play and the last man in.
And it's not for the sake of a ribboned coat
Or the selfish hope of a season's fame;
His captain's hand on his shoulder smote,
'Play up, play up,' and play the game.

> *Vitae Lampada*
> Sir Henry Newbolt
> 1862–1938

The Club enjoyed a revival for a few years in the mid 1970s, with much local success.

FOOTBALL

Teams from Ilsington and Liverton have enjoyed long and successful years on the football field, the latter being particularly strong during the 1980s and 90s. Though traditionally a man's game, women's teams have also been founded as the pictures opposite show.

Liverton FC 1947. Back row: 1. Bill Holcombe, 2. Harold Osborne, 3. Cyril Warren. Middle row: 1. Walter Sampson, 2. Len Paddon, 3. Bill Towell. Front: 1. R. Harris, 2. Derek Towell, 3. Len Richards, 4. Dick Cornish, 5. G. Williams.

Ilsington Football team, early 1970s. Back row: 1. Bob Cornish, 2. unknown, 3. Alan Jones, 4. Stephen Shaw, 5. Roger Carpenter, 6 and 7 unknown. 8. Gerry Towell. Front row: 1. Brian Towell, 2. unknown, 3. Raymond Honeywill, 4. Sam Leaman.

Ilsington ladies football team. Back row: Sonia Bowden, 2. Hazel Knapman, 3. ? Giles, 4. Margaret Squire, 5. Elsie Leaman, 6. Rosemary Christophers, 7. unknown, 8. Carol Heathman, 9. Stephanie Shaw. Front row: 1. Avril Knapman, 2. Val Williams, 3. Bariah Lacey, 4. Margaret Lacey, 5. Leslie Turpin, 6. Jennifer Cornish, 7. Isabel Shaw.

ILSINGTON, Near Bovey Tracey

TWENTY-FIFTH ANNUAL

FETE, FLOWER SHOW and GYMKHANA

(A real Old Fashioned Devonshire Show and Sports)

WILL BE HELD

IN A FIELD AT LIVERTON

ON

SATURDAY, JULY 29th, 1939

from 2 p.m. to 7 p.m.

PROGRAMME OF PONY SHOW and GYMKHANA

3 P.M.

	1st s. d.	2nd s. d.	3rd s. d.
Best Hack (any height) -	20 0	10 0	5 0
Best Pony (14 hands and under)	15 0	7 6	5 0
To be ridden by Children under 15			
Jumping (Open) -	Silver Cup	15 0	10 0
Children Jumping (Children under 15)	Silver Cup	15 0	7 6
Umbrella Race - -	15 0	7 6	5 0
Bending Race - -	15 0	7 6	5 0
Novelty Race - -	15 0	7 6	5 0

A SILVER Cup presented by Mrs. W. J. ALLEN

will be given for the Greatest Number of Points obtained in the Horse Events.

ALL HORSE EVENTS ARE OPEN—Entrance Fee 1/- each event, to be paid to the Gymkhana Secretary, W. J. Allen, Haytor Riding School, Haytor, Newton Abbot. Telephone : Haytor 261 (or on the Field).

The Committee do not hold themselves responsible for any accidents to Competitors or Horses.

SPECIAL CLASSES FOR BABIES and DOGS

Knock-Out DARTS COMPETITION (Open)

At 6 p.m. 1001 UP. Entrance Fee 2/- per team of 8.

To be handed in by 5-30 p.m. to Mr. S. W. A. GILL.

PRIZES : £2 FIRST PRIZE £1 SECOND PRIZE

NUMEROUS EXCITING SIDE SHOWS, TEAS AND OTHER REFRESHMENTS

Entrance to Field 1/- (Including Tax). Car Park 1/-

C. F. WILLS, General Secretary.

Telephone, Haytor 243

ILSINGTON FLOWER SHOW

The Ilsington Parish Flower Show and Fete was founded in 1910 by the Rev. J.D.H. Patch shortly after he arrived in the parish as Vicar of Ilsington in 1908. He found that the parish was deeply split between the Higher Side of Ilsington Village and Haytor Vale, and the Lower Side of Liverton, Halford and South Knighton, and his idea was to invite the two parts to participate in this annual event in late July. The idea worked very well particularly in the years between the two World Wars when extra classes for poultry, dogs, cats and babies were added.

The shows were held alternatively at Liverton and Ilsington, and later included Haytor Vale as a third venue. In those days there were some very keen gardeners in the parish, some almost professionals, who earned their living by gardening, and competition between them was very strong. During the past 15 years or so, interest has certainly waned and unfortunately the venue has now decreased to one, and the show is held at Ilsington every year.

Some new life is needed for the show for it to exist into the third millennium and I make a plea to everyone in the parish to see that it does.

ILSINGTON SHEEPDOG TRIALS

The first Ilsington Sheepdog Trials were held in 1950 to raise money to complete the parish war memorials. It was agreed that any money left over should go to start a village hall fund for the village of Ilsington.

It was one of the first sheepdog trials to be held in this part of England and was a great success thanks to the number of parishioners who rallied around to work for it, and the sum of £50 was available to start the nucleus of the village hall. At that time the Ilsington Schoolroom was the only available place for a dance or a large gathering.

That winter the Ilsington Parish Sports Society was formed with its objects to promote sheepdog trials, entertainment and sports annually in the parish for charitable purposes. Again the trials in 1951 were a great success and Ilsington was put on the sheepdog trial map as the organisers of the West of England and Devon County championships. A large committee of parishioners worked together admirably and it was everyone's aim to get a village hall for Ilsington as quickly as possible. Year after year the trials did well, the Ilsington Sheepdog Trials became quite a social event held annually on the first Saturday in September and, as our rival society the Devon and Exmoor Sheepdog Society put it in 1976, 'we remember the wonderful way in which the first Ilsington Sheepdog Trials helped to rally farmers and shepherds to take greater interest in their dogs and to benefit socially in the get-together of trials. We hope and believe that there will always be an Ilsington and we hold great respect for the Ilsington Sheepdog Trials.'

By 1961 the land for the village hall was purchased and the following year there was enough money raised to start with the building of the hall which was opened in October 1962. From then, and for nearly 40 years after, the profits from the trials were donated to the hall funds towards its maintenance. It has been a great success and asset for the village.

Sadly with the death of Herbert Whitley in 1998, who had been chairman of the trials almost from its beginning and who lent Halshanger Meadow for its venue for many years, and many of the sheep, the committee found themselves without a suitable field. Profits had been decreasing too, through the years, and the enthusiasm of local people to run it, although the number of shepherds and dogs had actually increased. It was therefore decided in 1999 after the 50th trials had been held, to call it a day.

SPORTS GALORE

Was it nineteen or twenty? Stan Cornish scratching his head when loading sheep into the lorry at Ilsington Sheepdog Trials. His daughter Judy is not sure either!

Right: *South Devon point-to-point races held on Haytor Down, 1929.*

Below: *Crowds gather to help a competitor at one of the early Simms Hill Motor Trials, c.1923.*

SPORTS GALORE

Ilsington Parish Fete and Flower Show Committee, 1910. T.H. Lyon (Middlecott) in centre, third row. Rev. J.D.H. Patch to his right. Also present are Harry Nickols, Oliver Roberts, Elias Manley and Mr K. Flower.

Ilsington Youth Club 1960s. Back row: 1. unknown, 2. Brian Towell, 3. John Roberts. Standing: 1. Derek Honeywill (with bat), 2. Cyril Honeywill, 3. Barry Squire, 4 – 6. unknown, 7. Cyril Giles, 8. Gerry Towell, 9. Ray Honeywill, 10. David Brown, 11. Bernard Saunders. Sitting: 1. Heather Edwards, 2 and 3, unknown, 4. Margaret Aggett, 5. Val Aggett.

Carpenters Arms Darts Team. Back row: 1. Reg Giles, 2. Sid Grose, 3. Harry Mortimore, 4. unknown, 5. Alf Head, 6. Bill Jeffries, 7. Fred Derges, 8. Charlie Derges, 9. Len Dymond, 10. George Derges, 11-14. unknown, 15. Oliver Roberts. Front row: 1. unknown, 2. Reg Tozer, 3. Ike Sanders, 4. Jack Dart (Landlord), 5. Eli Bourne, 6. unknown, 7. Jim Harvey.

An 'Any Questions?' evening at Ilsington Village Hall, October 1963. Front row l-r: Miss D. Passmore, B. Dunsford, Margaret Hurst, unknown, Mrs C. Retallick. Also in the picture are Mrs Gilpin, Mrs R. Smith, Peter Klinkenberg, Mr and Mrs A. Ware, Mr and Mrs Bryant and Norman Penellum.

A group of walkers who were beating the bounds of Ilsington parish in 1967. The location is near Chipley, by the old round house. They are: 1. Frank Petty, 2. Mrs E, Smith (Parish Clerk), 3. Valerie Frost, 4. unknown, 5. Alan Cleave, 6. Rev. John Donaldson (Vicar), 7. Horace Hawkins, 8. Dick Wills, 9. Bim Shenton, 10. Arthur Courtier, 11. Alan Phillpotts, 12. Roger Courtier, 13. Seymour Madge, 14. David Courtier, 15. Paul Rothwell, 16. Vivienne Frost, 17. unknown, 18. Blyth Shenton, 19. John Donaldson Jnr, 20. Yvonne Donaldson, 21. David Petty, 22. Philip Cleave, 23. Michael Donaldson, 24. Mary Donaldson, 25. Rodney Cleave, 26. unknown, 27. Kevin Hall, 28. Adrian Frost, 29. unknown, 30. Carol Donaldson.

Checking the parish boundary on the map, 1967. Adults l-r: Bill Blinston (Headteacher Blackpool Primary School), Dick Wills (Chairman PC), John Donaldson (Vicar), and Aileen Carrett.

5 - Beating the Bounds

The following extract was written by Bill Blinston, following the completion of the first Beating of the Bounds of the parish for 116 years, in 1967.

Following the line of the boundary as closely as we could, we crossed over the middle of the traffic island at Drumbridges, much to the curiosity of passing motorists, and finally made our way through the triangular shaped Pitt's Plantation, heather covered, with young shoots of honeysuckle sprouting everywhere, to the Exeter Cross–Stover road where Seymour Madge signalled the completion of the project with a fanfare on his horn.

A fitting end to an historic occasion awaited us at Liverton Village Hall where tables laden with food of all kinds had been prepared by a hard working band of ladies of the Women's Institute. As we did justice to the first class fare provided, I was able to officially declare that the ceremony had been completed satisfactorily and could report to the Parish that the boundaries are true and intact. Special tribute was paid to Dick Wills, whose knowledge of parish affairs and local history had worthily earned him the title of 'Mr Ilsington'. A walking stick which had been presented to him on behalf of his fellow parish councillors just before the first section of the bounds had been beaten in October '67; had accompanied him on all four excursions and is already a collector's piece.

Others came in for honourable mention; Harold Laver, vice-chairman of the Parish Council had completed the whole of the course, as did also his fellow Rural District Councillor Horace Hawkins, whose wife Betty was the only woman to qualify for this honour; Seymour Madge had led us around the course with his hunting horn, which surely should now be added to the Parish Archives; fifteen-year-old Paul Rothwell from Teigngrace, with his poodle Bunty, was the only outsider to do all four sections; Parish Councillor and moorland farmer, Arthur Courtier, celebrated his final walk by having his sons David and Roger and his seven-year-old grandson, Nicholas to accompany him – a great honour to have had three generations of one family taking part.

The only complete family on this last section was that of the Donaldsons. The Vicar, one of that honoured band of fourteen who had braved the moorland gale in the Leighon Valley in October '67 had taken part in all four walks, and his family of Carol (14), Yvonne (12), John (10), Michael (8), Mary (5) – as well as Mrs Donaldson (age undisclosed) and Rusty the dog had a record to be proud of. What a feat it was for five-year-old Mary to complete the walk without having to be helped. Hers was the honour of being the youngest person to take part in any of the four sections

Kevin Hall (10) had the doubtful distinction of being the only person to fall into a bog, but it hadn't dampened his enthusiasm for, with his brother Brian (12), he had taken part in three of the four walks. Other young people to do this were Vivienne (12) and Adrian (10) Frost, Colin Buckpitt (10) from Bickington, and Philip (11) and Rodney (9) Cleave. Enthusiast, Frank Petty and his nine-year-old son, David, from Ipplepen also completed three sections. It was pleasant to have the company once again of former chairman of Bickington Parish Council, Bertie Christophers and Mrs. Christophers, and we wish them luck in their coming retirement to Teignmouth. Two others who had been at the start of all four perambulations, and although unable to accompany us on those walks had certainly been with us in spirit, were there to greet us at the end; they were 'mother' of the Parish Council, Miss Passmore, and the Parish Clerk Mr R.M. Smith. Many others were involved but I hope they will forgive me if I do not mention them all by name – the list would be too long.

To me the most outstanding feature of the Bound Beating had been the warmth of the fellowship and friendship displayed among the people who took part; people from all parts of the parish and from outside it. I was particularly pleased by the number of youngsters who came along, for this is their heritage.

It is 116 years since the last time this ceremony took place. I hope you won't leave it so long before it is decided to do it again. I should like to take part but I doubt if I'll be in such good shape by that time. I should like to thank everyone for their support and especially Dick Wills for all his expert knowledge and help.

Bill Blinston,
Chairman Parish Council

Bickington beating their bounds in 1965. Bill Blinston is being bumped against the boundary stone on Ramshorn Down, the boundary against Ilsington parish.

Below: *Setting off past Hemsworthy Gate during the beating of Ilsington parish bounds in 1967.*

Left: *Dick Wills pointing out the first boundary marker, the Prince Albert stone, on Haytor Down, with his presentation walking stick, 1967.*

Left: *The Horseshoe Stone in the Becka Brook was lost for many years and thought to have been washed away by a flood. Found in 1997 by Jim Churchward it proves to be a feldspar marking in a granite boulder, and is most unusual. Previous searchers had been looking for a stone shaped like a horseshoe. It is mentioned in the 1566 survey of Ilsington Manor as a boundary stone.*

Below: *Dick Wills is bumped against an Ilsington parish boundary marker during the 1967 beating of the bounds.*

Left: *Walkers set off down Green Lane during the beating of Ilsington parish bounds to celebrate the centenary of the foundation of Parish Councils in 1994.*

The chimney stack at Silverbrook Mine. It was said that in 1852 an old man living in the parish had heard his grandfather say that Silverbrook mine had been abandoned in a hurry about 1757 by sudden flooding and the miners left behind them all their tools (which he enumerated). He said where these would be found if the mine was ever worked again and added that at the bottom of the mine there was a course of lead ore 'as big as a hogshead'. In November 1852 a 20-inch cylinder pumping engine was installed at Silverbrook being the first steam engine ever erected in the Ashburton area. On draining the mine the tools were found exactly as the old man had predicted. Clearing the sink brought to light two sets of wooden handpumps. When Silverbrook was closed, this steam engine was installed at Liverton Mill to augment the water-wheel there and is said to have been the cause of the disastrous fire in the 1900s.

6 - Mines and Mining

In the middle of the last century the first visitors were coming to Haytor especially to see the views and to appreciate the beauty of the open moor and its historical significance. Before that the moorland was considered a wasteland, of use to only a few who were prepared to quarry or mine it, dig peat, or graze their cattle upon it. Old William Honeywill the Ilsington sexton at that time summed it up by saying 'What people can see in they old rocks, I dawn't know!'

But Mr G. Henwood writing in a mining journal in the late 1850s exhorted travellers to climb to the top of Haytor Rocks and to witness the great extent of the ancient 'old mens' mining operations which stretched from here to Newton Abbot. He said a mine at Bagtor was worth a visit. Here modern miners had taken advantage of the workings provided by the 'old men', digging new levels below their old works and finding fine loads of tin. A huge water-wheel 60 ft in diameter had been constructed.

A few years ago another writer in the same journal said no trace could be found of this gigantic wheel, nor of the light railway which ran from Bagtor to Hemsworthy Gate for 1¾ miles. Remains can be seen of the breached dam near the source of the River Sig, known to the locals as Smallamoors, and the great T-shaped depression on the hillside above known as Pisky Pits, of which Henwood wrote 'The immense quantity of Mother Earth removed thence, will convince the sceptical that tin to a vast amount must have been obtained.'

Silverbrook mine working in the 1850s. Ilsington church tower can just be glimpsed on the left.

A second view of Silverbrook mine in the 1850s. Water was carried on wooden launders to drive the stamps to crush the ore-bearing rock and to work the buddles which helped separate the ore from the rock.

The 'old men' referred to by Henwood and others were those miners who sank the earliest shafts dating back in the 15th or even the 13th century. Their mines were drained by the 'rag and chain' method, bundles of rags tied to an endless chain at intervals. Before that the moor was dug in the open-cast method and examples of this can be seen in most Dartmoor valleys today where the land beside the rivers has been turned upside down in search of ore.

Crownley Works, above Bagtor Mill, the bounds of which were recorded in 1690 were worked, with Bagtor and Hemsworthy Mines, in 1845 as Haytor Consols. The Duke of Somerset and Lord Cranstown of Bagtor Manor spent £12–£14 thousand pounds on its dressing floors, buildings, workshops, waterwheels, stamps, a steam engine and the railway, before a ton of ore had been raised. Ten years later the mine was severely criticized as being 'Laid out regardless of expense, but then worked in a feeble and incompetent manner.'

THE BRIMLEY MANGANESE MINE

Some years ago in the 1930s I can remember a hole appearing in the ground in Brimley Orchard, behind the cottages. Looking down this hole a tunnel could be seen, but except for it being a convenient place to bury a sheep's carcass noth-

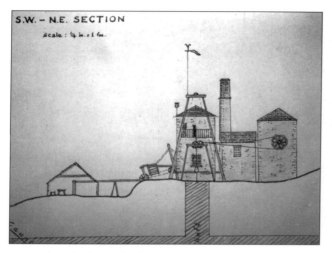

A sectional view of Silverbrook mine, drawn by John Somers Cocks.

ing more was thought of it, and it was filled in. In 1967 another subsidence occurred and an underground passage could be seen again. This time a young caving enthusiast, Robin Hood, was in the area and I asked him to have a look at it.

Equipped with mining gear and a field telephone he and a friend entered this tunnel but could get no further than the earlier subsidence. Robin's father excavated this blockage, sheep and all, and the tunnel was found to continue. With press reporters present, Robin and his friend,

Zaim, entered it, and it was found to be generally 5½ feet high and 3 feet wide, passing through bands of clay, sometimes red and sometimes white, with the solid rock of red Brimley-type chert intermingled with volcanic lava of some ancient volcano.

Nearly 100 yards along the tunnel were found drill holes bored into the walls, plugged with pieces of wood, bits of candles and fragments of drills and nails, almost eaten away by rust. Veins of manganese could be seen in the rock. Further on a shaft could be seen going up towards the surface. This had been blocked with stones but fresh air could be felt filtering down.

MOORSTONE

Moorstone, as the granite blocks and boulders lying on the surface of the moor were called, was used in vast quantities for all kinds of building from the 15th to the 19th century. Any convenient stones were used, especially near the roads, and consequently many ancient monuments of the early inhabitants of the moor succumbed to the hammer and chisel. At Smallacombe Rocks one can see that many boulders have been drilled and split, and one huge rock, complete with its rock basin, has been thrown down and now lies upside down.

Cottages at Lewthorne Cross, Ilsington, built by Alfred Lyon of Middlecott for Mine Captain William Grose and workers at the Atlas tin mine and Smallacombe iron mines.

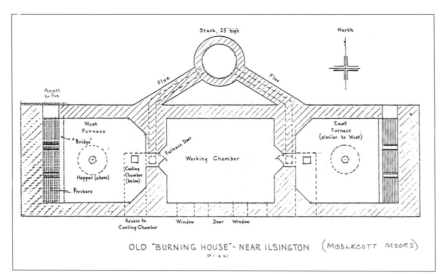

OLD "BURNING HOUSE"- NEAR ILSINGTON (MIDDLECOTT MOORS)

P.G.H. Richardson, noted writer on mining matters in Devon provided the following notes on the old 'Burning House' near Ilsington, now the property of Arthur Courtier.

Now that it is getting increasingly difficult to find above-ground mining features in South Devon which amount to more than mere rubble heaps, some details of the old burning house at Albion Mine, Ilsington, may be of interest.

This feature, situated on private land at Haytor has, due to its current use as a hay barn, survived almost intact, as shown on the accompanying drawing. The building, flues and adjoining 25-foot stack, are built of local stone, the building and stack being in a good state of preservation (though the latter is probably held together by the ivy) but the flues from the furnaces to the stack have crumbled somewhat.

The twin furnaces are of the reverbatory type, where the charge does not come into direct contact with the fuel used for firing (the firebars – shown in the drawing for the sake of clarity – have in fact been removed), ore from the stores above being shovelled into the shallow hoppers and so down to the furnace hearths below. The roasting ore would have been rabbled with long-handled implements inserted from the working chamber through the furnace doors, and when sufficiently roasted would have been raked into the holes leading to the cooling chambers below. This roasting of ore often formed a part of the ore-dressing sequence and was done partly to drive off unwanted constituents and partly to render the ore more amenable to subsequent processes.

It is hard to put a date on the building, but it could have been built in the eighteen seventies or eighties and probably continued in intermittent use until the early nineteen hundreds, though mining activity in the immediate vicinity continued rather longer – almost certainly until the early twenties.

There are several interesting and/or puzzling items, one of the latter being the relationship between the flues leading to the detached 25-foot stack and those leading vertically to the two ridge stacks on the roof of the building, and the absence of any dampers to control the flow of furnace gases between the two sets of flues. But in general the building as a whole presents a textbook picture, rendering the functioning of this type of furnace very easy to understand.

Above left: *William Grose (1838–1915), Mine Captain at Lewthorne and Trumpeter.* Centre: *Jill, Alan, Joyce and Garth Grose, descendants of William Grose, at Owlacombe Mine, Sigford, 1931.* Above right: *Mrs Emily Grose (1838–1927), William's wife.*

Early views in the 1820s of Haytor Granite Quarry with (left) cottages situated near the quarry on the moor, and (right) the blacksmith's shop with its huge bellows, and cranes and pulleys for loading granite on to wagons.

In his memoirs of Ilsington Jack Corrick mentions working on the slopes of Rippon Tor as a boy, dressing moorstone for kerb-stones. Shortly after the opening of the Granite Railway in 1820, George Templer was negotiating with persons who wished to use the railway for carrying away 'patent paving stones.' Moorstone was used for millstones (still to be seen at Smallacombe) for roller-mills, for crushing apples (some still in situ at Narracombe), as vats to receive the apple juice from the pounds, as staddles upon which granaries and corn-ricks were built (such a granary existed at Bagtor Barton until a few years ago), for the pillars of open sheds and linhays, for water troughs, bridges, farm rollers, querns, cheese-presses, gate-posts and a host of other things.

Throughout Ilsington parish there are still hundreds of these gate-posts in daily use, although in the past ten years many have been replaced because farm machinery is now so wide and stone posts will not accommodate modern gates. The earliest gates were of the slip-bar variety and their stone posts can often be seen. The most common are the slot-and-L-kind, with post holes cut in one post and an inverted slot in the other. Bars were then slotted between the two posts to act as a gate.

Stone posts can be dated roughly by the way they were split from the parent stone. Since about 1800 stones have been split by means of drilling a series of round holes a few inches apart and then hammering tares and feathers, kinds of wedges into the holes. Before 1800 the method of cleaving made use of wide wedges which leave a series of long depressions along the edge of the stone. Most gate-posts visible today were split by this latter method. Buildings and houses can also be dated roughly by this means.

Remains of the granite 'rails' on the Haytor railway along which wagons drew thousands of tons of stone from the quarry to the Stover canal at Teigngrace, on to the River Teign at Newton Abbot, and thence to Teignmouth where it was loaded on ships bound for London.

Haytor granite quarry showing the crane intact, c.1920.

It is perhaps surprising that although most of the 7843 acres of the parish of Ilsington are within the Dartmoor National Park, and that Haytor Rocks and Rippon Tor lie within its boundaries, only about a fifth of its area actually lies on the granite, the area where granite is naturally found. This means that every granite stone built into walls of houses, into hedges of fields, gate-posts, troughs or the hundreds of fragments lying around the remaining four-fifths part of some 6200 acres, all have been brought there by man. Perhaps this would not be such a tremendous feat today, accustomed as we are to giant earth movers and bulldozers, but the fact is that the vast majority of them got there on the backs of pack-horse or in small carts.

Quarrying for granite was almost unknown on Dartmoor earlier than the first part of the 19th century when Haytor and Foggintor (in Walkhampton) quarries were opened. Before that time surface granite was used, known throughout the moor as moorstone. Thus we have in the Rev. Philip Nansons' own words when he drew up a terrier or inventory of church property in 1727: 'the Vicarage House at Ilsington is built partly of slate stones and partly of moorstone.'

Moorstone has been used for building purposes from time immemorial. It was used in the hut walls of the Bronze Age such as those on Horridge Common and Smallacombe Rocks, and in the walls of their tiny fields which surrounded them.

Haytor granite was used in the construction of many of the capital's major buildings, including London Bridge, here at its opening in 1837.

The same people used it for ritual monuments and burial sites: the stone rows, barrows, tumuli, and cists (there are tumuli or burial mounds on Rippon Tor and Black Hill). It is unlikely however that moorstone was moved very far for these purposes, it being found around the site.

Unfortunately all traces of contemporary building off the granite, at Owlacombe Barrow, Lounston and Lenda, and no doubt many other places, have long since disappeared. From the 8th to 9th century onwards, in the building of the earliest farmsteads on the Dartmoor fringes, moorstone was used in their rubble walls, and roughly cut and dressed as corner stones.

Ingsdon quarrymen digging out stone from Ingsdon Limestone Quarry in the 1920s for road surfacing. During the First World War the roads and lanes of Ilsington parish became very bad. It was also the time when the lanes built for horse-drawn traffic were altered to accommodate motor vehicles, with the camber changed to a flatter surface. Quantities of stone were dug from local quarries (New Road Quarry, Silverbrook, Ramshorn Down etc.), cracked (broken up) by hand into pieces about four inches around for laying on the roads to be compressed by steamroller, or sometimes simply by passing traffic! In the picture are (top) the Nicholls brothers, (bottom l-r) Frank Blackler (grandfather of Roy Blackler), 'Brassy' Roberts (grandfather of Jack), Alex Roberts (father of May Honeywill), 'Uncle' Ned Cox, the Council Surveyor (name unknown), Jack Blackler (Uncle of Roy Blackler), and Jack, son of Alex Roberts who was to be killed in the Great War.

Where the surface of the land had to be cleared of moorstone boulders they were used in building the boundary walls of new fields. Away from the granite area farmsteads were built from the stone found there or, where this was in short supply or unsuitable, cob and wood were used. Even in these places hearths and corner-stones had to be constructed of a stone that could be worked, and so they had to import moorstone.

Except for these special uses for moorstone and its occasional use for fonts from the close of the 12th century, granite was not used in any appreciable amount for building until the 15th century. It was then used in large quantities in the widespread rebuilding and enlargement of churches.

Look at Ilsington church. The tower was built at the end of the 15th century almost completely of granite. Can you imagine how many cart loads were brought from Haytor Down? Each stone had to be squared and given a face side; what a feat with only a hammer and chisel. Now go to the east side, to the outside wall of the chancel. Here at the south-east corner you will see that the quoin or corner stones are not granite, denoting that this part of the church was built before the 15th century: instead they are red and yellow sandstone very likely brought all the way from east Devon. The porch, built about the same time as the tower, has granite quoins infilled with brownish-blue slate stones from the village quarry in Middlecott Wood. But where did the magnificent pillars of the nave arcade come from? Where were they carved and by whom? How were they brought to their present site? It certainly makes one think.

TRAVEL AND TRANSPORT

7 - Travel and Transport

Before the days of motorised transport the parish was criss-crossed by lanes which joined farms and cottages to the centre of the village and beyond to the outside world. The coming of the motorcar changed all this, not only bringing about the need for wider and better-surfaced roads, but bringing more and more people on to Dartmoor as holidaymakers. Marion Grant recalls the 1920s:

The first motor vehicle to make regular visits to Ilsington village, was when two enterprising young men from Liverton bought an old lorry. They were Sid and Wilfred Potter who worked very hard cutting down trees from the woods, and cutting them up into logs. On Saturday mornings they brought them around the village in their lorry and sold them.

After many months of this arduous work an idea occurred to them which would enable them to increase their income. After selling the logs they would brush off the lorry, put wooden seats around the three sides and an awning over the top, and in this 'home-made bus' the local people were invited, for a small fare, to book their seats and be taken to Newton Abbot and back on Saturday afternoon.

The bus left from the top of the village ('Up top village') at 2.00 pm and the return journey left Newton at 5.00 pm. As the engine of the vehicle was not very powerful and the New Road, leading up to the village was long and steep, the young and able-bodied alighted at the bottom of the hill and walked up. The elderly and the shopping were left on board and waited for the walkers at the top of the hill. Our very first public transport!

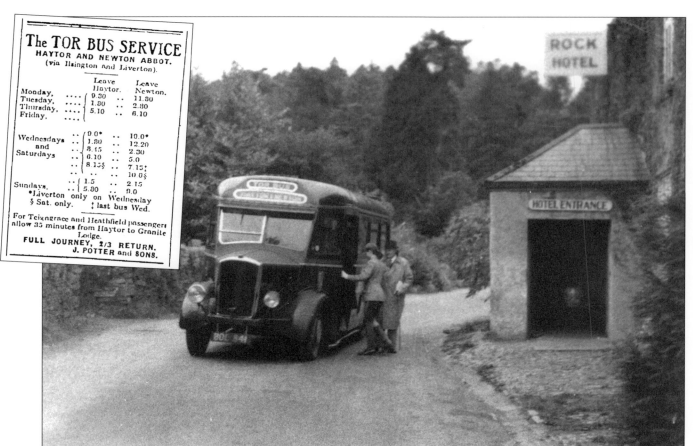

The Tor Bus Service outside the Rock Hotel in the 1930s.

Left: *Alfred Courtier (1893-1915) was killed at the battle of Loos in September 1915. Son of Joshua and Mary Ann Courtier of Ilsington, his brother, John Henry, was also killed in the Great War in October 1918.*

Above: *RAF Flt-Sgt Lewis Roberts (1922-45) and Jean York were married at Ilsington on 12 September 1944. He was killed four months later on a raid over Bergen in Norway.*

Ilsington Home Guard - A Company 5th Platoon, 1944. Back row l-r: *Arthur Honeywill, Ern Cornish, Harry Piper, Lew Giles, Raymond Smerdon, Alfred Smerdon, Jack Lloyd, Harry Jackson, Jack Carpenter.* Middle row: *Jack Woodman, Ike Saunders, Alan Cleave, George Northway, J. Geddes, Gilbert Roberts, H. Hannaford, Alf Harvey, George Baker, Herbert Whitley, Stan Cornish.* Front row: *Arthur Courtier, F. Connor, Charlie Coysh, Ron Coaker, Charlie Wills, Arthur Read, Alf Head, Seymour Madge, George Harvey, Jim Harvey.*

8 - Ilsington in Wartime

One of the earliest accounts of conflict in the parish comes from a Civil War tract of 1645 relating events that followed the Battle of Bovey Heath.

FROM 'A TRUE RELATION OF THE FIGHT AT BOVY-TRACY' BETWEEN PARLIAMENTS FORCES UNDER THE COMMAND OF SIR THOMAS FAIRFAX AND THREE REGIMENTS OF THE KINGS HORSE

PRINTED FOR EDW. HUSBAND, PRINTER OF THE HONORABLE HOUSE OF COMMONS. JAN. 15. 1645.

To the Honorable William Lenthall Esq. Speaker of the Honorable House of Commons. Sir, whilst Sir Hardres Waller, yesterday amused the enemy with a party of horse and foot near Okehampton, two regiments of foot and one of horse marched from Crediton to Bovy-Tracy, about 14 miles, and at 6 at night fell on three regiments of the enemy's horse at Bovy-Tracy, took near 400 horse and 5 colours, some prisoners, many escaping in the dark.
J.R. Moreton. Jan 10. 1645 9 a.m.

To the Honoured Edmund Prideaux Esq. Member of the House of Commons. Sir, We took at Bovy 400 horse at least, and 7 horse colours, whereof one is the Kings, having the crown and C. R. upon it. A major and some officers being in a house, shut the door, and threw out of a window about £10 in silver, which the foot soldiers were so busy about getting their shares, that the officers escaped in the meantime over the river through the darkness of the night. About six score (120) of those who escaped afoot, got into Ellington (Ilsington) church that night and sent to Lord Wentworth for relief. We drew out a party of horse and foot next morning to surprise them, but they footed it away to their other quarters and so escaped.

The army advanced the next day being Saturday to Ashburton, but the enemy having received a hot alarm by those that escaped, quit that place being their headquarters, in great confusion, sending their foot one way and their horse another, and our forlorn hope pursued them so fast through Ashburton that we took 20 horse and 9 prisoners.

Truly our soldiers march with that cheerfulness, as I have never seen them before in this service. The greatest inconvenience happens to the horse, by reason of the slippery-ness of the way, and little bridges of straw to be gotten for them. The enemy's horse are ill-shod, neither can they tell how to get them shod, which is an undoubted argument they dare not attempt to break through eastward at this season. The prisoners say they did not expect our motion this weather.

It was during the pursuit of the Royalist forces that the episode took place in which horses were stabled overnight in Ilsington church (see Chapter 2)

NAPOLEON'S LEGACY

At Liverton we have a building estate of houses erected about eighty years ago called Telegraph View. I wonder how many people today know the reason for this name? It is not, as I have heard some say 'There used to be telephone poles and wires along the road in front of the houses', but that the houses are facing Telegraph Hill, the hill on the sky-line to the right of Ingsdon Hill and behind the Welcome Stranger.

On October 31st 1805 Mr Roebuck, a civil engineer and Inspector of Telegraphs for the Admiralty, was ordered to select sites for a line of telegraph from London to Plymouth. There was a danger of an invasion by the French under Napoleon and there was a necessity of being able to send signals quickly. Mr Roebuck was told to use the existing telegraph stations from London to Portsmouth as far as he could. Two months later, after a rapid survey, his plans were approved and work on them began.

The first eight, out of ten stations to Portsmouth, were used. Then a chain of 22 stations to Plymouth. The Devon ones were at St Cyres near Honiton, Rockbeare Hill, Great Haldon, Telegraph Hill near South Knighton, Marley Lee near Ivybridge, Saltram, and Mount Wise. William George was moved with his family from the telegraph station at Sittingborne in Kent to be in charge of the new telegraph in Ilsington parish.

It is said that in exile on St Helena Napoleon dreamed that one day he would see the tricolour flying on Ilsington church tower. Had he lived another 150 years or so his dream would have come true, for the French flag was flown during the signing of the twinning charter with the people of Brasparts in 1976.

On July 4th 1806 Mr Roebuck was able to report that a reply had been received at the Admiralty in London from Plymouth in twenty minutes. Before long the one o'clock time signal could be made to Plymouth and its receipt acknowledged in only three minutes. The telegraph at this date worked on a shutter system invented by the Rev. Lord George Murray. Very rapid transmissions, only possible with simple arbitrary signals, were used, and the Admiralty steadfastly refused to replace spelling by codes.

In September 1814 after the defeat of Napoleon and when it was thought he was safely shut away on the island of Elba in the Mediterranean, the Plymouth line was closed down. The telescopes were returned to the Admiralty, the men given a month's notice and sacked.

The Ilsington Overseers now began to worry that they would have to keep William George and his family on the poor rates, perhaps for the rest of their lifetime, and consequently delved into records to find out his birthplace, which was

Bristol. Under the Elizabethan Poor Law System, still the law of the land after more than 200 years, the overseers of one's birthplace were responsible for one's relief in time of need.

So William George and his family departed for Bristol; Telegraph Hill returned to sheep and cattle, rabbits and buzzards. Time has passed by, the cottage and buildings have gone. Memories of William George and his telegraph have passed away.

COL. SEYMOUR HALE-MONRO 1856–1906
By Ian A Woodason

In the Lady Chapel is a memorial tablet dedicated to one of the Monro family of Ingsdon; Seymour Hale-Monro the only son of C. J. Hale-Monro. He entered the Army in August 1876 joining the 72nd Highland Regiment, and his first action was the second Afghan War of 1878-80. After conquering most of the country the British Army suffered a major defeat and the remnants fell back on the city of Kandahar where they were besieged. The 72nd Regiment under General Roberts were mobilised at Kabul to march on Kandahar 323 miles away with 18 000 soldiers. At the ensuing battle Monro was severely wounded but the siege was lifted. In 1881 under Army reforms the 72nd Regiment became the Seaforth Highlanders. Monro took part in the Egyptian war of 1882 again being mentioned in dispatches.

In 1886 he married Lady Constance Vaughan. Ten years of action on the N. W. Frontier of India followed, serving with the Chitral Relief Force in 1895 where a small British Garrison was besieged with the relief column having to navigate the deep snow of Shandur Pass at 12 000 feet. Next year he served on further campaigns on the N. W. Frontier including the Malakand campaign made famous by the young Winston Churchill.

At the outbreak of the Boer War in 1899 the Seaforths joined the Highland Brigade and took part in several battles. Monro was promoted to Colonel and again mentioned in dispatches. After the Peace of Vereeniging in 1902 he returned to India and was named C.B.E. When he died in 1906, aged 50, he was General Officer Commanding the Ahmadnager Brigade.

FLT. SGT. LEWIS ROBERTS

Recently I have helped Roger Perkins of Haytor write a booklet on the men of Ilsington who gave their lives in two World Wars and are commemorated on the war memorial tablets in Ilsington parish. His booklet has recently been published called *A Devon Parish at War* and he has given me permission to publish his findings on one parishioner who died, here. It is of Lewis Roberts whom I knew very well, who was about my age and with whom I went to school at Ilsington.

Born 1922 the eldest son of Sidney and Beatrice Roberts. He was husband of Jean Roberts of Highclere, Hampshire. Killed in action 12 January 1945, he is commemorated on the CWGC memorial at Runnymede (Panel 272).

After training at RAF Llandwrog Wales as a Wireless Operator/Air Gunner he joined the crew of F/Sgt Bradford for final training on four-engine bombers. He joined the elite 9 Squadron based at RAF Bardney, Lincolnshire and their first operations included attacks on the U-boat pens at La Pallice, France, and Ismuiden, Holland. The squadron was withdrawn from operations for re-equipment and their aircraft were modified to carry the 12 000lb Tallboy bomb developed by Barnes Wallis. At this time in September 1944 Lewis married Jean at St Michaels, Ilsington (she became a widow just 4 months later and their son David was born the following August).

The Tallboy was first used by 9 Squadron on 15 October when 18 Lancasters attempted to demolish the Sorpe Dam. Direct hits were made but the massive structure remained intact; no aircraft were lost. At the end of the month 37 Lancasters of 617 and 9 Squadrons flew north to Lossiemouth for another special operation. The 42 000 ton battleship *Tirpitz* had been spotted in Tromso Fjord, Norway. Carrying extra fuel for the 2250 miles round trip, the attacking force found the fjord covered with cloud. None of the 32 Tallboys dropped found their target: one aircraft failed to return which successfully crash landed in Sweden. Two weeks later the two squadrons made a second strike on Tromso this time in brilliant sunshine. Two Tallboys found their mark and the *Tirpitz*'s magazines exploded and she turned over.

The next operation in December was a night raid on Gdynia, Poland, to assist the advancing Russians and to destroy the pocket battleship *Lutzow*.

The New Year opened with a daylight trip to one of Germany's most heavily defended loca-

tions, the Dortmund–Ems canal. One of the Lancasters caught fire over the target and George Thompson the wireless operator, who Lewis must have known well, was awarded a posthumous VC in trying to save the crew. On 12 January, Lewis' tenth operational sortie 32 Lancasters were sent in daylight to attack with Tallboys the concrete U-boat pens in the harbour of Bergen, Norway. Four Lancasters were shot down over the target, Lewis' aircraft piloted by Flying Officer E.C. Redfern DFC was one of them. It crashed into the sea and none of the crew survived.

ILSINGTON HOME GUARD

The author's reflections on the Home Guard:

The Local Defence Volunteers (LDV) later called the Home Guard was formed in June 1940 after the evacuation from Dunkirk. There were two platoons in the parish one at Ilsington and the other at Liverton – Bickington had another. We had no uniform and no arms, we wore a khaki armband with the letters LDV on our arm, working clothes, and any weapons we could lay our hands on, shotguns, rifles, hay forks or just big sticks. It was decided that we should man a lookout for parachutists every night on Ramshorn Down and a roster was drawn up for two men together, to do stints of 2 hours on 4 hours off from 7pm to 7am, (6 men, 2 from each platoon).

At first we had a little tent and later a hut. Luckily nights passed off very peaceably except hearing and watching German aircraft passing over at times to bomb Plymouth, and we could even see in the glow in the sky when Bristol and South Wales were bombed. Nearby, the Langmead bull in the next field with a bell around his neck kept us alert, as well as Gipsy James and his family with their camp just below us, returning from the Jolly Sailor at kick-out time. An attraction were the hundreds and thousands of glow-worms all around in those warm summer nights, a sight I had never seen before or since.

By day of course the Home Guard were always on the alert and in the evening attended courses, rifle practices, and at weekends exercises with the army. Eventually we got our guns and ammunition and our uniforms.

Ilsington Parish Council celebrating the Golden Wedding Anniversary of Mr and Mrs Ern Cox of Rora Farm. He was PC Chairman for many years. Seated l-r: Herbert Brockway, Dick Wills, Dorothy Passmore, Ern Cox, Mrs Cox, Arthur Courtier, Harold Retallick. Standing: F. Woolway, Mrs Brockway, Mollie Wills, Mrs Blinston, unknown, Bill Blinston, Yvonne Ware, Alex Ware, Horace Hawkins, Rev. John Donaldson, Anne Donaldson, Ron Smith, Clare Retallick, Charlie Colwill, Mrs Smith, Betty Hawkins, Harry Starkey.

Presentation of the Chain of Office to Ilsington Parish Council by Lt-Col. L.C. Pitman, 1963. Back row l-r: Dick Wills, Arthur Courtier, Harold Retallick, Alex Ware, Norman Roberts, Charles Colwill, Jack Carpenter, Ron Smith (Clerk). Seated: Herbert Brockway, Horace Hawkins, Lt-Col. Pitman, Bert Bryant, Dorothy Passmore.

9 - The Parish Council

The forerunner of the Ilsington Parish Council was the vestry meetings, the earliest records of which date from March 1827. Meetings were held fortnightly and dealt with various matters arising in the parish, including the provision of monies and clothing etc. to the parish poor. Such money was raised through the Parish Poor Rate exacted on all property owners.

Other matters covered in Vestry meetings included the upkeep of roads and bridges, health and sanitary issues, and education.

The first meeting of the Ilsington Parish Council was held in the Ilsington Schoolroom on Monday 31 December 1894. The council had been newly appointed and consisted of:

Capt. C.J.H. Monro (Ingsdon)
R. Alford (Brimley)
J. Cumming (Wood Cottages)
M. Cumming (Lower Sigford)
C. Ellis (Liverton)
W. Grose (Lewthorn)
W. Lambshead Sen. (Portland Villa)
W. Lambshead Junr. (Honeywell)
G. Tarr (Ilsington)
W. Thorn (Ingsdon Mill)
C.W. Wills (Narracombe)

The first officers to be elected were:

Chairman – W. Lambshead Sen.
Vice chairman – W. Grose
Honorary Clerk – J. Cumming

The first subject to be discussed by the council was regarding the enclosure of a piece of land known as the Haytor Vale Village Green. As the council said 'it has never been enclosed since the cottages in the Vale were built about 80 years ago, and it has been freely used as a playing-ground by the public since then. Now the lord of the manor, of Ilsington, Preb. R.R. Wolfe of Leighon, has fenced it around.' The reply from Preb. Wolfe was as follows: 'I beg to state that the houses of Haytor Vale are not public property but private. The piece of land is not a village green. The village of Haytor Vale has always been, and still is, the private property of one individual person. The roads leading to the Vale are also his private property and repaired by him. The public have no right whatsoever to use these roads except under sufferance. The piece of land has been enclosed because pigs and horses strayed upon it and became a nuisance. The enclosure was made before the Local Government Act 1894, came into being.'

Several times in the next few years Preb. Wolfe was asked to repair his roads from Ludgate and Two Posts (Cottamoor Cross) to the Vale, and later the District Council was asked to adopt them, but nothing happened before the turn of the century. Parish footpaths were also frequently discussed in those early days, as they were still being used by parishioners going to and from work.

The Church Path from Smallacombe to Haytor Vale was reported in a bad state, especially after Mr Lyon's workmen had drawn timber from his property.

Mr Alford requested that the path from Woodhouse to the top of Town Hill be repaired, and it was decided to erect notices forbidding its use by riders.

Bovey Tracey parish council was asked to have the name Haytor engraved on the stone direction post at Five Wyches Cross 'to prevent strangers from taking the wrong road to Haytor.'

The Clerk was instructed to take names of those willing to give evidence respecting the paths through Great Plantation or the Wilderness. A committee met Mr St Maur, the owner, and it was agreed with him there were two public paths, one from Cummings Cross to the Bovey–Newton Road for Heathfield Works, and the other to the top of Sandypool Hill. Other footpaths mentioned were: 'A rail required for the footbridge leading to Woodgate Cottages so that no-one can walk into the brook,' and one from Halford to Rora.

Soon after its first meeting the council arranged with Mr Beare to hire the room at Liverton for all council meetings and also for the purpose of paying the poor and for vaccinations. Later a platform was erected so that the room could be used for concerts.

The early council was very much concerned with allotments and not only a strip of vegetable garden was meant, but also fields for smallholdings. Ilsington Village was asking for three acres of pasture and one of arable, and a field was required at Sigford Cottages for Mr. R Aplin. The Ilsington charities were asked for two fields at Halford, one for allotments and the other for recreation. Mr Tickle required a field at Coxland Bridge. The old allotment field at Rora, owned by Mr Woosman, was eventually taken over by the council. At Ilsington one of the glebe fields was offered by the vicar, the Rev. T. Hale, but farmer Bill Rowell of Town Barton was the tenant. Many letters went to and fro regarding his tenancy valuation and in the end the council asked him to suggest an independent valuer. True to his character, determined to have the last word, farmer Bill replied with this pungent riposte. 'Will you kindly ask your Chairman what he thinks is a fair compensation, as I always think he is a good judge of other people's business.'

Presentation to Arthur and Lily Courtier on their Golden Wedding Anniversary by Ilsington Parish Council, 1988. Yvonne Ware, Dick Wills, Christine Lamb, Nancy Cleave, Horace Hawkins, Arthur Courtier, Jack Elliott, Barry Lacey, Fred Saunders, Lily Courtier, Roy Paver.

10 - Twinning

Twinning towns and villages in the UK with ones of similar size in France was popular in the 1970s.

Meetings were held at Ilsington, a twinning committee was formed and we picked Brasparts, a parish of approximately the same size of Ilsington situated in the hills of mid-Brittany, some 30 miles south of Roscoff, and a small deputation was sent there. Five of us who went received a warm welcome and we spent a weekend in the homes of our hosts. A party from Brasparts paid Ilsington a visit shortly afterwards, and the result was that we decided to twin.

As the Mayor of Brasparts, M. Pierre Cras, put it: 'We have visited each others homes, met the family; we have liked what we have seen and decided that a marriage shall take place.'

Our first official visit to Brasparts, which included Ted Ashman, chairman of the Ilsington Parish Council, and his wife, Mrs Yvonne Ware, Susan Ware, Mr and Mrs Philip Gibson, Mr and Mrs Horace Hawkins, Miss Sylvia Miners, Sydney

Ilsington residents and French friends on a twinning exchange visit a supermarket near Brasparts. Left to right: *Marie Le Corre, Susan Wills, Marcel Perrot, Remy Perrot, Evelyn Adamson, Marcel Le Corre, Beryl Alford and Sydney Reed.*

Reed, and the author as secretary, took place in July 1976. We attended their Fête du Cheval, their annual horse festival, and on July 11th 1976 Ted Ashman signed the Ilsington–Brasparts Twinning Charter. Each of us stayed in the homes of our guests: language seemed no barrier, although they told us 'Our native language is Breton. We only speak French when you came over.'

That September a party from Brasparts visited Ilsington, and a duplicate charter was signed at the Ilsington Sheepdog Trials on 4 September 1976. During the next 14 years many visits were made between the two villages and many friends made between the two communities. Teams of footballers played each other for a rose bowl and teams of petanque (boules) for a cup, and many places and entertainments were enjoyed in Brittany and Devon. Just recently visits have only been made by footballers.

Later it was agreed to twin with Ste Marguerite d'Elle in Normandy as a second place, and twinning visits are regularly held between there and Ilsington.

The ancient church at Ilsington's twin town, Brasparts.

HAPPY FAMILIES

MRS. FOX.
THE PARSON'S WIFE

MR TARR, THE PUBLICAN

MR. BOWN, THE
MUSICIAN

MR GILES, THE SEXTON

MR GROSE
THE
MINER.

MR. HEATHMAN, THE
CARPENTER.

MR. WREYFORD
THE FARMER

MISS GILES
THE SEXTON'S DAUGHTER

When my fathers' generation at Narracombe were growing up, in the early years of the 20th century, they played Happy Families with a 'pack of cards' they drew of Ilsington characters.

There were twelve occupations of four cards each, drawn by one of my aunts, with the captions printed by my father, and most were very good likenesses of the individuals. Particularly good were Mrs Fox, the parson's wife, who walked daily around the village in the winter months with her can of soup for the poor and aged; George Tarr the stout publican of the Carpenters Arms with his quart of cider; Middy Bown on the church organ; Jockey Giles the sexton walking around the village with his hands clasped under the tail of his coat; Capt. Grose with his miners' pick, captain of the local Atlas Mine at Lewthorn; Winky Heathman, born at Winkleigh, the carpenter; the poor farmer Sam Wreyford with his skinny calf, and last but not least the poor daughter of Jockey Giles who was 'in the decline.'

11 - Ilsington Characters

Beneath those rugged elms, that yew-tree's shade,
where heaves the turf in many a mouldering heap,
each in his narrow cell for ever laid,
the rude forefathers of the hamlet sleep.
The breezy call of incense breathing morn,
the swallow twittering from the straw-built shed,
the cocks' shrill clarion, or the echoing horn,
no more shall rouse them from their lowly bed.

For them no more the blazing hearth shall burn,
or busy housewife ply her evening care.
No children run to lisp their sires' return,
or climb his knees, the envied kiss to share.
One morn I miss'd him on the custom'd hill,
along the heath, and near his favourite tree:
another came: nor yet beside the rill,
nor up the lawn, nor at the wood was he.

From *Elegy written in a Country*
Churchyard by Thomas Gray (1716–1771)

JOHN FORD

John Ford the dramatist was born at Bagtor House and baptized at Ilsington on 12 April 1586 by the vicar, the Rev. George Sweete. He studied at Oxford, matriculating at Exeter College in 1601. In 1602 he entered Middle Temple, but was expelled from there for debt and was not re-admitted. In 1606 at the age of 20 he produced *Fame's Memorial, or The Honoured life, peaceful end, solemn funeral of the Earl of Devonshire.* Also *Honour Triumphant* and *Monarchs' Meeting: the King of Denmark's welcome to England.* Was Ford influenced by what he knew as a boy of Charles Blount, Lord Mountjoy and Penelope Devereux living at the cottage next to his family's estate?

In 1663 *'Tis a Pity She's a Whore* was acted at the Phoenix Theatre in Drury Lane and the same year *The Broken Heart, Fide Honour* and *Lovers Sacrifice.*

In 1638 Ford produced a masterful chronicle play *Perkin Warbeck,* and the following year *The Lady's Trial.* After this at the age of 52 he dropped from sight, but it is said he returned to Devon to end his days. Where Ford retired to is not known. He may have returned to Bagtor to live with his maiden sisters Jane and Elizabeth, or to Sigford with his bachelor brother Thomas, or even to

Mountjoy Cottage. We do know that he was not buried at Ilsington, for there is no record in the church registers.

MRS COLLINS OF SILVERBROOK

Marion Grant tells the story of an old lady who lived alone in the cottage of Silverbrook Mine, in the wooded valley below Ilsington Village:

When my grandmother, Mrs George Tarr, was land-lady at the Carpenters Arms an old lady called Mrs Collins who lived in a cottage amid the ruins of Silverbrook Mine buildings came up through the woods every evening to the off-licence pigeon-hole carrying a large blue jug. She didn't go into the public bar but went to the cubby-hole, a small window with a shelf, on which she would knock with her jug. Mother usually served her. 'A ha'pence worth of beer, me dear' she would say. The weather never stopped her, pitch dark, blowing a gale, pouring with rain, deep snow or sweltering heat, she still came. One very stormy winter's night she was there as usual. Mother gently suggested to her 'Why not take a penny-worth tonight, then you won't have to come tomorrow in this dreadful weather.' 'But I likes coming, me dear,' she replied 'the wither don't bother me. You'm the only person I sees all day.'

Inevitably there came the night when she didn't turn up, neither the next night, or the night after that. Mother became worried, and she and her brother decided to go down to investigate. They found the old lady dead in her bed with the blue jug at her bedside, the beer untouched.

BILL ROBERTS.

One of the two brothers who at harvest-time called themselves 'Roberts Brothers, hay lifters and cider shifters'. Bill was well in his seventies and was making his way home from the Carpenters Arms, when one of the first aeroplanes flew over the village. 'How d'ye like to be up there, Bill?' one of the youngsters said to him. Bill stopped and looked up and quick as lightning answered 'I'd sooner be up there in 'im, than up there without 'im!'

JOSEPH DENLEY 1809–91
(told by Harry Denley)

In the year 1819 when my grandfather, Joseph Denley was just ten years old he was bound apprentice by his parents to Mr Charles Corbyn Wills of Town Barton or 'King Charlie' as he was generally known. The life of a farm apprentice in those days was hard and their conditions entirely depended on the goodness of their master. Farmers were forced to have a number of apprentices compared to the size of their farm, and some had as many as 6 to 8 at a time, their ages ranging from 7 to 20. A large part of the drudgery of the farm work of those days was done by them, their life was long hours of work often with little food, their clothing only what was passed on from one apprentice to another, and no pay. They had to work or got the boot or the stick, no back answers in those days. However grandfather soon learnt his father's trade, thatching hay-ricks and corn-ricks, then barns and sheds and later houses.

My grandfather Joseph Denley went from being a farm labourer to Haytor Granite Works to work as a labourer. It was about 1829 and London Bridge was being built from Haytor granite. Later he became landlord of the Carpenters Arms and had several horses and carts which he and his sons used for hauling granite from Haytor to Torquay for the building of chapels and churches. He brewed his own beer. Granny or Betsy used to weave straw baskets to carry primroses and other flowers. When they left the Carpenters Arms they went to live in the bottom cottage facing Honeywill Lane.

GEORGE PROUSE 1841–97
(by Harry Denley)

Lived in the bottom cottage. He was a pensioner from the Queen's Life Guards. When his pension was due he got a 4¹/₂ gallon of beer, propped it up on the end of the table and he would empty it before he left. It would have cost him half a crown. Next door was Mrs Bickley and her son Phil and next door again Old Sam Giles, they called 'Jockey', a good tempered old boy who was sexton at the church. At that time he was boss of the boys at Atlas Mines at Trumpeter, who worked on the floors, the stamps and the buddles where the tin was extracted from the ore. I can tell you, old Jockey had something to get on with, with all those boys. Quite a number of miners came from Cornwall and others from Ashburton, the latter walking to work and back every day. Mrs Denley

and her daughter Mrs Wills lived in the cottage opposite Town Barton farmhouse. They were scared stiff of thunder and lightning. They would hide in the cupboard, but us kids would rattle the doors to frighten them some more.

BERT FROST

The long-legged driver of the Tor Bus for many years. Nothing was too much trouble for Bert; old people would stop the bus anywhere on the way from Haytor to Newton, via Heathfield and Teigngrace, and give him a slip of paper to get tablets or medicine from the doctor's surgery, or do some shopping for them. Good-natured Bert never refused and went all over town to get their needs, and bring it back on the return bus for them. His motto was 'always room for one more' and the Tor bus used to groan its way out of Newton, sometimes stopping on the outskirts to take on more if he thought there were inspectors on the look out for over-crowding around the bus station. Before starting off from Newton he would look around his passengers to see if Mrs so-and-so was there. We must wait for her, he would say, and perhaps after 10 minutes or so there she would be, loaded up with shopping and puffing and blowing, to say she was held up in a queue.

MR AND MRS BILL BALL

They lived in No. 3 St Michaels Cottages. He had been a carpenter born in the parish and they were married at Bickington Parish Church by the Rev. Thornton on 29 August 1858. Mrs Bell was formerly Elizabeth Furze. They celebrated their golden wedding in 1918 when they had 8 children, 28 grandchildren, and 22 great-grandchildren, and in 1928 they celebrated their diamond wedding. All their children had emigrated to America except one son, Fred, who lived at Christow.

There is a story told that Mrs Ball went to visit her children in America for a six-month stay. Her husband was at work when she arrived home at her cottage. When he got back from work all he had to say to her was 'Is my tea ready, missus?'!

They died within a few days of each other in May 1931, she 91 he 94.

ERN ROWELL b.1877

Born at Liverton. He left school at 14 years for his first job of tending the white-hot furnaces of Stormsdown and Owlacombe tin and arsenic mines, walking 7 miles to and from work. The ore

CHARACTERS

At the Star Inn, Liverton c.1912. The landlord's son Ernest Doddridge was to be killed in the Great War.

The Star Inn in the 1890s. The two people seated in the doorway are Elizabeth and Samuel Doddridge (the landlord and his wife).

Carpenters Arms outing, 1925. Back l-r: Harry Nickols, Bill Derges (both worked at Narracombe Farm). Front: Bill Redstone, charabanc driver, Ern Carpenter (landlord).

Jim Harvey Snr of Coxland, Sigford (1860–1936).

Ilsington bellringers' outing c.1925. Included are Andrew Harvey, Laudy Roberts, Eli Bourne, Fred Derges, Jim Harvey, Jim Harvey Snr, George Harvey, Alf Northway, Bill Flay, Oliver Roberts.

was baked in great ovens after it had been crushed by 5 ton hammers and it had to be turned regularly, otherwise it clogged. Arsenic was different. It was laid down like white soot on the sides of a ¼ mile flue by the fumes which passed along it, and to gather it you had to crawl along the flue with your ears and nostrils blocked, and scrape it off.

For two years he went clay-mining in Canada. He had heard old miners talk of a manganese mine in Penn Wood called Mount Pisca, and remembers being told that lead cannon balls had been dug up there. He always said that 'Dartmoor ought to be developed. Nobody knows what riches are there.'

CAPT. C. H. QUELCH

Retired to Ilsington in 1936, after being a speculative builder in London, he built a bungalow at Birchanger Cross. In 1938 when nearly all the cottages in Ilsington Village had been condemned by the rural council as unfit for human habitation, he purchased the lot and obtaining a housing authority grant, he rebuilt them and re-let them to the villagers.

Several cob built cottages were totally demolished except for their chimneys. Afterwards he did the same at Trumpeter.

PHAROAH GROSE

Tin and arsenic mines of Owlacombe have been silent since the early 1920s. Pharoah married in January 1896 in America and then followed a lifetime of mining in Devon, USA and India. Born at Trumpeter July 1867, he first went to a dame school, and when Ilsington School was built in 1873 was one of its first pupils. At the age of 13 he left and went to work at Haytor Iron Mines managed by his father Capt. William Grose. For two years he worked in the blacksmith's shop taking sharpened drills to the miners in the mines.

Sometimes he walked in front of the traction engine which carried the ore down to Bovey Tracey where it went by train to the smelting yard in the North. Someone had to walk in front of the new-fangled road machine with a red flag; Pharoah was only too glad to volunteer for the duty. Mining was already a dying industry in the west, and Pharoah went to work in shipbuilding at Dartmouth. He came back to mining, to the lignite mines at Bovey and then a lead mine in Yorkshire. At the age of 22, in 1889, he returned to Ilsington to the Atlas Mine until it closed down three years later (1892). He emigrated to America. There he met his future wife Annie Jeffrey, who came from Cornwall. They met in Michigan, USA and married there, but Mrs Grose did not like the climate of her adopted country and they returned to England where Pharoah obtained a job in the iron mines at Brixham in charge of work underground. That job lasted six years and then he moved to Owlacombe where he was assembling machinery for the new plant. This lasted 4 years but again he was out of a job and, leaving his wife at Owlacombe to look after their children, he went to the Kolar gold fields in India. For 16 years he stayed there, coming home on furlough every three years. In 1930 he returned to Owlacombe and retirement.

JOCKEY GILES 1844–1922

One of the best known stories about Jockey Giles still told today, although it happened nearly a hundred years ago, tells of a hot summer's Wednesday when he was sexton and 'Passon Patch' had gone to Newton to market.

Jockey was tidying up the churchyard when he suddenly remembered that he should have told the vicar that an old parishioner at Haytor had died. He had dug the grave but he had not informed the vicar when the funeral service was needed and the time of the funeral was near. What could he do?

He ran as fast as he could up the road towards Haytor, but when he got to Lewthorn Cross he could see the walking procession carrying the coffin coming around the corner down the road towards him. Shouting as loud as he could 'Go back, go back, you can't be buried today, the parson's gone to Newton.'

Poor old Jockey never heard the end of it. For years after, children used to call after him 'go back, go back, the Parson's gone to Newton'!

Another story used to be told of Jockey Giles, the sexton. Whilst he was digging a grave in the churchyard (remember in those days it was the practice to re-bury in the same ground time and time again) he suddenly shouted 'Here's old — 's skull, 'e never 'xpected to see the light o'day again'! When the undertaker visited him regarding a funeral he said to him 'Whilst you'm here, you just as well come upstairs and measure up the ol' woman, 'er can't last long.'

Jockey used to wear an old fustian coat, and walked about with his hands clasped behind his back. Old Sid Grose could copy him to a tee.

GEORGE TEMPLER 1781–1843

George Templer of Stover, who was at one time part Lord of the Manor of Ilsington, and Master of the South Devon Hunt, 1810–1826, brought home a tame monkey home from India. He used to dress this monkey up in full hunting pink, and when he was hunting took it with him mounted on another horse.

One day when hunting he lost his hounds and stopping to inquire at a cottage from one of his tenants he asked the old lady if she had seen the hounds come that way. After much curtsying she replied 'Yes, zer, they came pass 'yer a few minutes ago and your son was riding after 'em, like the very devil'!

FATHER ROGER FOX

Roger Fox, son of a vicar of the parish, recalls events in Ilsington around the time of the Boer War. One Christmas, it must have been 1900, I was given a tambourine. A few months later I was on the knees of a nurse in the schoolroom at Ilsington which was quite full. Hermon Davies was going around the room with my tambourine whilst all the people, with mother playing the piano, were singing: 'When you've shouted Rule Britannia, When you've sung God Save the Queen, When you've finished killing Kruger with your mouth. Will you kindly drop a shilling in my little tambourine, for a gentleman in khaki ordered south.'

MEMOIRS OF MRS CASEY

In 1967 I [the author] saw in the local newspaper that a Mrs Elizabeth Casey of Torquay had just celebrated her 102nd birthday, and that she had lived for many years in Ilsington parish. Not knowing anything about her, I visited her and was most surprised to hear the details of her life.

When the Rev. Robert Lovett became Vicar of Ilsington in 1867, Mrs Caseys' father, Samuel Heale, came to Ilsington to help him farm the Glebe. The family lived in the cottage, now the Ilsington Post Office, which in those days had a yard and farm buildings attached.

She said, 'there used to be doors to the pews in the church and the children used to sit in the rising seats at the back of the church. At the top of these seats was the organ, with the choir in seats around it.' She remembered the laying of the foundation stone of Ilsington School in 1872 and was one of its first scholars. The vicars' wife, Mrs Lovett was a little old lady with a grey Quakers' shawl, pinned with a brooch. Mr Lovett was a kind man but very strict, who spent most of the winter months at Torquay, with a curate at

Ilsington. Mrs Casey's father planted the row of beech trees beside the road for Mr Lovett to protect his new walled garden. Mrs Casey also remembered having to fetch water from the shute (which still exists today in Cherry Trees wall at the top of the village) in buckets, and when that dried up from the spring in the field towards Simms Hill.

When Mr Lovett left Ilsington, the author's great-grandfather Dr Braim came to Ilsington, and, asked if she remembered him, she replied: 'Too well. He did not farm the Glebe as his predecessor had done, so her father became coachman and gardener.'

Mrs Casey was in the choir from the age of 10, and her brothers Harry and Lewis blew the organ and were ringers. When she was 12 she left school and went out to work. In 1880 when the author's grandparents were married she came to Narracombe with them. She was here when my father and his twin sister were born the following year, and she carried him about for miles, for the roads were not fit for prams in those days.

'I remember your great-grandfather George Wills (1813-1893) very well, he used to get the gout very badly, and you had to look out when he had his gout boots on! I also remember your other great-grandfather, Dr Braim, who was vicar of Ilsington. He asked me to tell him where Brazil was. As quick as lighting I said "In that bag, sir" pointing to a bag in his hand. He replied "It isn't quite what I meant, but very good indeed, very sharp," and he gave me two Brazil nuts in each of my little hands. The village boys used to wait for Dr Braim walking home from Church, and go to meet him. He would ask them questions, but he never let them go without giving them a halfpenny each, which he used to carry in his waistcoat pocket. Off they would go, down to the village shop, and get two sticks of peppermint rock for a half-penny.'

Of modern Ilsington she said 'What a difference, I wouldn't mind living there now. It is nice to see all those old shutes gone where we had to collect water in buckets. The bones in my wrist are still crooked from having to carry heavy buckets of water every day when I was little.'

RICHARD LEARE

The author has an arithmetic book which belonged to his six-times great-grandfather, Richard Leare, who farmed Narracombe (the farm which he farms today in Ilsington parish), three centuries ago. This fragile book of some 65 pages was presented to young Richard Leare in 1696 when he was 21 by his former schoolmaster John Cruse of Bovey Tracey, perhaps as one of his best pupils showing him all his schemes of work.

Richard Leare was the eldest son of Thomas Leare of Narracombe who married Elizabeth Rowell at Ilsington on January 14th, 1674. He was baptised at Ilsington on February 17th, 1675. His father, who was copyholder of his ancestor's farm at Narracombe (it was part of the estate of the Manor of Ilsington, owned by the Ford family) purchased the freehold of the farm whilst Richard was growing up.

In 1702 on October 8th, when he was 27, Richard married a distant cousin (it was the custom amongst my family to marry distant cousins to stop the land and money leaving the family), Joan Wills, a daughter of George Wills of Rudge Farm, Lustleigh, at Lustleigh Church. A marriage settlement was drawn up to provide for Joan's welfare should she be widowed and for Richard's father and mother in retirement. An inventory shows that the Narracombe was stocked with 200 ewes and lambs, 16 bullocks, 10 acres of wheat, barley, oats and peas, 6 pigs and 2 horses. Thomas Leare, his father, died in 1717 and was buried at Ilsington on April 3rd, and his mother on March 23rd, 1723.

At Manaton Church on December 31st, 1728, Richard and Joan's only son Thomas married Elizabeth Nosworthy, another distant cousin, the eldest daughter of Oliver and Dorothy Nosworthy of Torhill and Neadon Farms in Manaton parish. Once again a marriage settlement was drawn up as a family insurance. Richard now aged 53 handed over the running of the farm to his son Thomas, and retired to the cottage in the courtyard at Narracombe. But all was not well. Perhaps Thomas, an only son, had had things too easy in his youth. His farming did not prosper and he had to resort to extortionate moneylenders. Within ten years he had come to the end of his tether and his father had to step in to save the farm. He took over all of Thomas' stock which was 5 cows, 7 young bullocks, 4 calves, 6 horses, 1 colt, 89 wether sheep, 47 ewes, 32 lambs, and 9 pigs, and in return paid all his debts. Richard did not long survive this upset and on June 23rd, 1743, aged 68, he was buried in Ilsington churchyard. Unfortunately his grave is unmarked today.

During his life Richard Leare was closely concerned with events in Ilsington parish. He served for several terms as churchwarden, as a member of the parish vestry, as overseer, as an official of the

Pages from Richard Leare's arithmetic book.

court leets, of the local commons of Haytor Down, and Ilsington and Bovey Heathfields, and as one of the original executors and first trustee of William Candy's Charity.

His arithmetic book, compiled by schoolmaster John Cruse, and completely written by hand, shows that foreign money was circulating in this area at that time and that local trade was conducted in a mixture of English, French, Spanish and Portuguese coinages. We learn that an angell was the name for a 50p piece, an inch is three barlicornes, a French crowne is six shillings, and that 12 riolls make a crowne, 5 souses make a rioll, and 12 denares make a souse. That in an alternative French monetary system a liver equals two shillings and that 20 souses make a liver and that 10 Portuguese riolls make a ducatt and 40 rees a rioll, and that 11 Spanish riolls make a ducatt and 34 marmeeds make a rioll.

Questions are set such as 'There was a roper married his daughter to a soper and gave with her in marriage 24 ropes and every rope had 24 knots and every knot had 24 purses and in every purse was 24 pence. The question is how much the roper gave with his daughter for her marriage portion?'

Another questions asks 'If a staff of 3 foot in length be sett directly upright cast a shadow of 7 foot in length, what height is that steeple which casteth a shadow at ye same instant 192 feet in length?' And 'If an ounce of saffron costs 4s 9d what will 19lb 10oz cost, and how many peck of wheat at 11 shillings the peck will pay for the same?'

The front cover of the arithmetic book is decorated with scrolls and stylised motifs of angels and birds and on the back cover Richard has written the births and baptisms of his children all born at Narracombe and baptised in the same font at Ilsington Church where all the rest of us have been baptised. Susannah born August 6th, 1703, baptised August 26th; Thomas born February 9th, 1705, baptised February 26th; Joan baptised August 10th, 1710; Mary born June 5th, 1715, baptised June 21st; and Elizabeth his granddaughter born January 10th, 1729, baptised February 2nd.

At the back of the book there are tables of the rateable values of all the Devon parishes arranged in their hundreds. Ilsington is valued at £124.17.9d, Bickington £78, Bovey £193, Ashburton £239.

I now possess three personal articles of the Leare family: a pine Bible box carved with an arrowhead border enclosing roundels and the stylised bird motif; a brass studded box which belonged to Richard's grand-daughter Elizabeth, dated 1748; and this book. There is their large oak-panelled clothes press upstairs, the turnspit-jack, and numerous documents of their conveyances, marriage settlements, fines, wills etc. among the Narracombe deeds, but their greatest gift to me is the house and soil of their ancestral home: Narracombe.

REV. J.D.H. PATCH'S MEMOIRS and THINGS WHICH GO BUMP IN THE NIGHT

When Rev. Patch came to Ilsington as vicar in 1908 there were many parishioners who would not dare to venture far after dusk. Stories of strange nocturnal happenings were commonplace and treated as very real.

There was the reckless coach and horses with the headless coachman of Birchanger Hill, the big black dog near Lenda Gate which often caused horses to shy when they passed that spot, the procession of horsemen down Green Lane preceeded with riders in white garments carrying lighted candles or torches, the shouts of 'rope rope rope rope' from the deserted mine at Silverbrook.

Mr Patch tells of a Mr Vincent who lived at Bagtor Mill. In his words 'He had been spending the evening at one of the cottages in the village. In due course he departed for home accompanied by his dog, and the household locked up and went to bed. They had not been long there when a frantic knocking at the door roused them and on opening it they found Mr Vincent as white as a sheet and begging to be allowed to remain for the night. His tale was that he had not gone far past the chapel before he found the road completely blocked with woolpacks and a voice bid him depart before anything happened to him. His dog meanwhile had given a frightened yelp and disappeared through the hedge and was seen no more. Next morning nothing was to be seen at the spot.'

Then there were the little twins dressed in white, standing hand-in-hand at Middlecott gate, the pig with a chain on its leg at Narracombe Brook and strange happenings at Bagtor House. Several years ago Mr Edward Bovey of Buckfastleigh whose family, the Widgers, lived at Sigford House for many years, told me that it was supposed to be haunted by an old woman looking for a hoard of gold under one of the hearths. He said the Widgers had had all the hearths up at one time or other, but never found anything.

In the opinion of Mr Patch these stories had their origin in the days when smuggling was carried out around these parts, this could have been tin or brandy. Smugglers were not at all anxious to have people wandering about at night and staged these apparitions to keep them indoors.

But what of the story of Mrs F. B. Roberts of Little Stapleton, which occurred only a few years ago and which she told to the author. She had a friend staying with her with two small children, and one fine afternoon in the middle of summer they went out for a walk. Suddenly in a narrow part of the lane leading from Smokey Cross towards the moor, now usually called Miss Feary's Lane, she heard something approaching her at a fearful rate. Looking up she saw in the distance a coach and horses coming towards her at breakneck speed, rocking from side to side on the rough road surface and taking the whole width of the lane. Desperately she grabbed her two children and leapt into the hedge, hoping that somehow the runaway coach would get past her. But it never came. It had disappeared into thin air, and it was just a pleasant summers' afternoon.

MEMOIRS OF JACK CORRICK

We used to round-up the ponies on the moor every year for the owners to claim their foals. We would ride out over the moor and bring all the ponies down to Pinchaford Newtake where Jasper Lambshead lived. Farmers would bring their branding irons and brand their ponies with their initials, some on the hoof, some on the side.

We had another good time when it was swaling time and we went up on the moor to burn the gorse or fuzz. Some of us boys would be on one hill, some on the other and we would see who could make the biggest blaze.

At Westabrook Farm we got plenty of callers, George Taylor, the estate carpenter, came to lunch one day. He opened up his bag and took out a two-pound loaf and some meat and cheese. Mrs Tickell gave him a two-quart jug of cider. He cleared the lot. Old Thatcher Bray would call and stop yarning until 11pm and then had to walk home to Blackaton, the other side of Rowden Gate on Dartmoor. The butcher came here from Bovey, his name was Bovey. He always came on Thursdays and would let his horse out of the trap for a feed and a rest. Mr Bovey always had dinner with us, and took all our dairy products, eggs, rabbits, poultry or anything that was going.

MR. BOVEY, THE BUTCHER.

Mr Corrick goes on: 'I was born at Honeywell Farm and I started school when I was four. My teacher was Miss Jessie Clark and the school master was Mr Heathman, a very powerful man. When I left the infant class and came under him 'in the big room' things didn't seem rosy. He was a very strict man and one of those chaps who didn't tell you a second time and didn't begrudge giving us the cane. The big boys from Liverton who went to Blackpool school, had to come to Ilsington when they got to a certain age, as they only had a woman teacher at Blackpool, and they were always in trouble before they got to know Mr Heathman.

After I left Farmer Tom Lambshead at Alston I got a job with Farmer Bill Rowell of Town Barton, Ilsington. He used to call every boy 'Cockey' and the first thing he said to me was 'Have you passed all your standards at school?' I replied 'Yes sir'. Then he said 'Have you passed the meat standard?' 'No, sir' I said. Then he said 'Come with me.' We went into the kitchen and he cut me off a couple of slices of bread around the loaf, and a huge slice of meat from a round of beef, put it between the bread and said 'Eat that, Cockey and then you will have passed the meat standard.'

MEMOIRS OF LES MANLEY

Haymans Cottages in Liverton were built by Edwin Cummings of Ilsington for Henry Beares' works at Liverton in the 1850s, also his dwelling house. He was drawn to the area by John Divett owner of the potteries at Bovey Tracey, who was building up a landed estate in the area, and very interested in water power building water wheels to drive machinery. Hand made bricks were made on the Ilsington and Bovey Heathfields, with sand from Blackpool copse, weathered clays from the Heathfields, lime from the kilns.

Walking home to Liverton from Newton Abbot with my two old maiden aunts when I was a small boy, they would clutch my hands tighter and tell me to hurry along when we got near Exeter Cross or we would hear the bones of the men hanging on the gibbets rattling. What a more likely spot could there be for a highwayman's gibbet, at a four cross road on the London-to-Plymouth highway, in the middle of a desolate heathland as it was then. Memories might even have reached back to the unfortunate young blacksmith of Ilsington, Tom Campion, who was hanged on the Heathfield in 1795 for his part in the bread riot at Bellamarsh Mills, Chudleigh (see over).

'MY COUSIN SUSIE'
(MRS SUSIE HARVEY, NÉE BICKFORD)

I always tell people that we (I mean the Wills family) have only moved 5 miles in 500 years, when they start boasting about where they have been. Some old villagers did not move very far. The story was always told me by my father's cousin Susie that when my great-grandfather George Wills went to South Knighton on his retirement in 1880 there was an old man there called Bill, who was heard to say one day 'I've never been out awver' (meaning he had never been over the moor). Grandfather said to him, 'When us go out with the wagons in the Fall to get vearns (Grandfather always spoke to the men like my Father did, in dialect), us'll take 'ee with us, Bill.' The time to collect ferns from the moor came, for bedding animals, and Bill went with them for the day. When they got back Grandfather asked him how he liked it. 'Thank Gawd us be back in England again, wance more' was his only reply.

When she was living at Devon House, Bovey, in the 1950s an old man called Smerdon had some fields around and a small flock of sheep, she said to him 'How are your sheep, Shepherd?' He replied, 'I ban't the shepherd, I be the owner.'

Another time she heard that one of his ewes had died, and she said to him 'I'm sorry to hear that you have lost a sheep, Mr Smerdon' he replied, 'I ain't loss 'im, I knows where 'e is. 'Es' up under the 'edge, daid.'

BILL AND ELIZABETH BALL

Bill Ball, the village carpenter, lived with his wife in one of Tudor Cottages, the one next to the Church entrance (they are called St Michael's Cottages today). There was a small patch of garden in front of the cottage surrounded by a low white-washed wall and on summer days 'Old Bill' could be seen sitting on this wall smoking his clay

THE ILSINGTON RIOT

A few years ago I heard that someone whose relations had emigrated from Ilsington to the United States early in the 19th century, was staying in a local hotel and wished to see me. On contacting them I found them to be Mr and Mrs Harlow from Houston, Texas, and that Mrs Harlow's great-grandfather was James Southward who had married Ann Gotham at Ilsington Church in 1794. My first words to her were 'So you've returned to expiate the crime of your forebear, William Southward, have you?'

I explained to her that at the end of the 18th century, just after the revolution across the Channel when thousands of members of the aristocracy and land-owning classes were guillotined and the mob took control of that country, there was a great deal of unrest around here. The price of bread, potatoes and basic foods soared to such a height that the average labourer was on the starvation level. There were rumours that flour was being exported to keep it scarce and expensive, and it is a fact that the General in charge of the troops in Plymouth wrote to London that there were 500 soldiers in the military hospital, many returned from the West Indies, who had no clothing and no pay. William Sunter, a J.P. of Ashburton, referring to a proposal to increase the number of French P.O.W.'s in the town, said there was a scarcity of food in the vicinity, owing to the Fleet lying so long in Torbay and the poor harvests of the previous year. He went on 'I am sure we shall have riots. I sent carts to Plymouth to try to buy corn, but they returned empty because corn was bought up by a combination of millers determined to keep prices artificially high'.

On the morning of Monday 13th April 1795, a large and well-planned mob from Ilsington and Bovey armed with clubs and axes, forcibly entered Bellamarsh Mill and destroyed a great part of the machinery and threatened instant death to those who opposed them. Mr James Ball, one of the proprietors, had met them on the road and endeavoured to dissuade them from their purpose, even offering them wheat at a cheap price, but in vain. A detachment of the Cornish Militia, quartered at Chudleigh, proceeded to the spot and seized one of the ringleaders, Thomas Campion, a young blacksmith from Ilsington, as well as two other Ilsington men, William Northway and William Southward, but a fourth, John Mortimore, evaded capture. Two days later when officers with a warrant for the arrest of John Mortimore visited Ilsington, they were forced to retire by a mob armed with various weapons which assembled there.

Before Judge Heath at the Exeter Assizes on August 1st, Thomas Campion, William Northway and William Southward all received sentences of death. It was alleged that they went about assembling a mob of upwards of 300 persons under the pretext of lowering the price of corn. It was said they carried a red and white flag, white for the avowal of French principles, and red that they would spill their blood in support of them. The parson of their parish expostulated with them to cease, but to no effect.

The Home Secretary, the Duke of Portland, commuted the sentences of death on Northway and Southward to one of seven years transportation to the colonies because there appeared to be a difference in the active parts they had taken. The Vicar of Bovey Tracey. the Rev. Joseph Dommett, himself a wrestler, pleaded for the life of Northway, saying that he had helped arrest him at Bellamarsh, and he was too good a wrestler to meet a felon's death'.

The sentence on Campion stood, although he had always before been respected by those who had any connection with him, they said he was sober, honest and industrious. He was sentenced to be hanged near the place of his crime. Both the Judge and the County Sheriff were insistent that the execution be expedited (five days instead of the usual fortnight) and that a military force be present because it was feared the local community would make a bid to rescue him. Campion was escorted to his place of execution on the Heathfield in sight of his parish church, guarded by a large contingent of troops which included a detachment of Artillery, two field pieces, two field officers and 300 rank and file from Roborough Camp, one captain and 60 rank and file from Berry Head Camp, and cavalry from the 26th Light Dragoons at Exeter.

The execution which was solemn and peaceable struck great awe in the minds of the spectators. His body was buried on Sunday, August 9th in an unmarked grave in Ilsington churchyard. In spite of offers of a Royal Pardon and money by Miller Ball, Mortimore was never apprehended. Northway and Southward disappeared into oblivion and no record can be found of their transportation. When I told Mrs Harlow this, she maintained that her family had served 188 years transportation to the colonies, and were due for restitution!

William and Elizabeth Ball of 3 St Michael's Cottages, with their daughters. He was the village carpenter.

at his white beard with one hand and then with the other, rub his stomach and say 'I'm not very well maid. Me beggerin' old evett ee've been rigglin' about all night!'

The story goes that many years before, on a hot day, walking home from work, Bill put his head under a shute of water coming through the hedge. When he had slaked his thirst from the pure Dartmoor water, he persuaded himself that he had swallowed an evett (whatever that was). For the rest of his life he believed the 'evett' was still inside him, that it would wait to eat the food he swallowed, and nothing would make him believe otherwise. He lived to the age of 94 so the evett couldn't have done him much harm.

Mrs Ball was a wonderful old lady. She always wore a white starched apron, a shawl around her bent shoulders, and on her white wispy hair a little lace cap, which was threaded with black ribbon on weekdays and a purple ribbon on Sundays.

SOME OTHER CHARACTERS OF NOTE

pipe. Mother would sometimes send me [Marion Sanders] to see if Mrs Ball wanted someone to fetch water for her. There was no water piped into their cottage and it had to be fetched in buckets from a tap across a wide causeway. Passing Mr Ball I would say to him 'Good Morning' and ask him how he was feeling. He would look at me with his rheumy eyes, take a drag at his old clay pipe, pull

Mr. Elias Manley of Belle Vue, Liverton, lived at Higher Brimley for 13 years as a boy and went to Ilsington School in the 1880s. Some years ago he told me several interesting items he could remember of those times:

Mr John Heathman was the Schoolmaster. He came from Chudleigh way and his wife was a Wills from Ideford. She had two brothers, John and George, who farmed at Lounston, and his niece, Miss Jessie Clark, was his assistant teacher.

The 'potwater' which ran in an open leat from

Ilsington women and girls make up a sewing party held at Narracombe around 1905.

Above left: George Tarr, landlord of the Carpenters Arms and blacksmith, with his wife Sarah (née Ford). She was a descendent of the ancient Ford family, Lords of the Manor of Ilsington and Bagtor. The photograph was taken in School Road, Ilsington, site of the demolished Manor House. Above right: Anna Jane Robson, eldest daughter of George and Sarah Tarr.

Haytor to Ilsington Village was the only supply of water. The watercourse divided just below where the Haytor Hotel is now, one part crossing the road and going through the Vicarage grounds and the Sanctuary and in an open gutter down past the school to the Carpenters Arms; the other following the road, flowing out the 'shute' at the top of the village, and then in an open gutter right down through the village towards Simms Hill. Children used to drink at the corner of the churchyard outside the school, lying on their stomachs.

There were two blacksmith's shops in Ilsington Village, Waldron's situated where 'The Old Forge' is now, and one adjoining the Carpenters Arms worked by George Tarr.

The well by the road at Higher Brimley was open, and to get water a bucket attached to a rope was thrown in. The water there used to dry up in the summertime and then they went to Lower Brimley, the spring at the bottom of Well Lane, Woodhouse Farm, Woodhouse Brook, or the spring up in Narracombe fields at Doxwell, for water. All some distance away.

There were a lot of people living at Higher Brimley in those days. Elias Manley well remembered the 'grand birthday' of Charlie Evans once every four years on Leap Day. Miners used to walk through Brimley every day on their way to and from work at Blue Waters Mine from Haytor Vale. There was a shop at Higher Brimley kept by Mrs Daymond. There was a lot of emigration and Mr Manley remembered the Hamlin family leaving their cottage in Back Lane for America.

12 - Hotels, Inns and Guesthouses

THE CARPENTER'S ARMS

At the end of the 18th and beginning of the 19th century Court Barton Farm was let by the owner Mrs Ann Hale of Ingsdon first to the Mudge family and later to Robert Petherbridge. When the latter's tenancy ended the farmland was taken over by Charles Corbyn Wills who farmed Town Barton, and as there was no need for the Court Barton farmhouse, it was put up for sale. This was eventually purchased by William Northway of Brimley, negotiating with Mr J.P. Carpenter, a relative and executor of Mrs Hale, and the old farmhouse was turned into a public house. William Northway named the new pub after the man who had helped him purchase it – The Carpenters Arms.

About this time the Parish Poor House was overflowing. The ancient parish brew house then named the Church House Inn occupied the upper storey, gained by steps, at the south end of the building. When the new public house came into

Above: *The Carpenters Arms c.1955 with the church in the background.*

Below: *Town Barton (built about 1875) and the Carpenters Arms. The photograph was taken c.1903. Note the row of elms along the churchyard wall. The sign reads 'Carpenters Arms, Ilsington.'*

being this was taken over by the Poor House, and as well a new Poor House was built on waste land near Smokey Cross.

THE WELCOME STRANGER

Built at the same time as the new turnpike in the 18th century and called the New Inn up to about 1960. I wonder whether the brewery who changed the name, knew of the significance of the new one, for from the church registers 'a foundling was baptized on 26.7.1772. who was dropped at the New Inn and left upon the parish.' She was given the name of Mary Inn. Happily to say she lived to the good old age of 84, married a local man William Coleman in 1793, and raised a large family.

THE STAR INN, LIVERTON

Originally the farmhouse of Cold East, farmed by the Shapleys for many years. When it is alleged 'that the Sportsman Arms by Benedicts Bridge on

the main Exeter–Plymouth road was closed by the owners of Stover House, because it was the centre of poaching on the Stover Estate', the licence was transferred to the Star Inn. Cold East Farmhouse was purchased about 1862 by William Mortimore of Ilsington, yeoman, from Samuel Shapley and it became a public house owned by Mortimore's Brewery of Kingskerswell for several years.

The Rock Hotel (or the Rock Inn) Haytor Vale, was originally built by George Templer of Stover to serve his cottages built as Haytor Buildings to house the quarrymen working at nearby Haytor granite quarries. Later in the nineteenth century these cottages became 'fashionable' dwellings and the Rock Hotel was much frequented. A Mr Joll from Bovey Tracey ran horse-drawn coach excursions on to the moor calling at the Rock for refreshments.

HOTELS AND GUESTHOUSES

MOORLAND HOTEL
HAYTOR ROCK.
HAYTOR HOTEL
ILSINGTON.

Two charming Holiday Hotels on the edge of the Moor, respectively 1,100 and 800 feet above the sea. Tennis, Croquet, Riding (hacks and ponies for hire). Electric light; central heating. Modern cuisine and service. Good Garages.

Stations: NEWTON ABBOT or BOVEY TRACEY.
Trains met by arrangement.

Telephone: Moorland Hotel, Haytor Vale 7.
Telephone: Haytor Hotel, Haytor Vale 14.

Proprietors: TRUST HOUSES, Ltd.

Ludgate House was designed by the architect Thomas Henry Lyon and built in the mid 1890s for Samuel Courtier and his wife to run as a hotel. The first visitors, a Mr and Mrs Lang of Hampstead, London arrived on June 4th 1897. Three visitors' books exist and the last entry is given in 1931. On the death of Mrs Courtier, Samuel sold Ludgate and built 'The Moors'. The new owners were Mr and Mrs Bradford of Pinchaford. In 1940-41 Ludgate House, Moorland, and Haytor Hotel (now Ilsington Country Hotel) were taken over, first by the War Dept as a battle school and subsequently by the Americans in 1944. Officers were billeted at Moorland, a demonstration platoon at Ludgate House, and NCOs at Haytor Hotel. The Ludgate Barns predate the building of Ludgate House.

The Moorland Hotel, Haytor was opened in May 1903 at a cost of about £3000. Demand from the growing tourist trade had outstripped the existing provision (Ludgate House) and access from Bovey Tracey had improved, with day trippers and longer-stay residents seeking refreshments and accommodation on the moor. The original owners, Messrs Hellier and Lee were formerly coaching proprietors of Bovey Tracey. The hotel originally had 17 bedrooms and stood in extensive grounds. The Moorland Hotel was severely damaged by fire in 1969 but reopened in December 1984. It was sold in 1998 to H.F. Holidays Ltd who undertook its refurbishment.

The picture on the left shows the Moorland in 1925 with Haytor in the background.

HOTELS AND GUESTHOUSES

The Moorland Hotel shortly before it was burnt down in 1969. It remained derelict until it was rebuilt in the mid 1980s.

The Haytor Hotel, Ilsington, now called the Ilsington Hotel, was originally opened in 1902.

Originally the Haytor Hotel, this is now the Ilsington Country Hotel. During the Second World War it was a school, and was later occupied by British and American soldiers.

HOTELS AND GUESTHOUSES

Left and below left: *The Haytor Tea Rooms were started in 1924 by Jack Allen who also ran the Moorland Stables. The original building was an ex-army hut put there after the First World War by Bob Bradford of Pinchaford, in Pinchaford Newtake.*

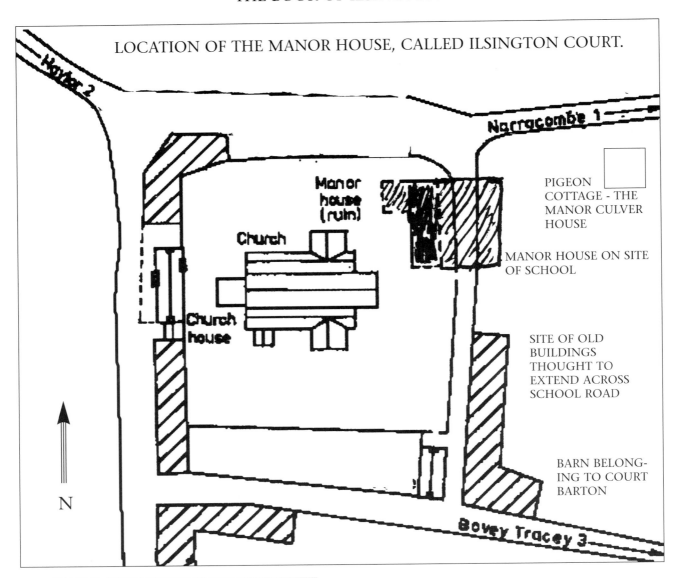

LOCATION OF THE MANOR HOUSE, CALLED ILSINGTON COURT.

Manor house (ruin)

Church

Church house

N

Haytor 2

Narracombe 1

Bovey Tracey 3

PIGEON COTTAGE - THE MANOR CULVER HOUSE

MANOR HOUSE ON SITE OF SCHOOL

SITE OF OLD BUILDINGS THOUGHT TO EXTEND ACROSS SCHOOL ROAD

BARN BELONG-ING TO COURT BARTON

The archway which stood in the churchyard at Ilsington was part of the ruins of the old Manor House. The arch fell down when a visitor swung on it.

13 - The Manor House

I have always been intrigued with the ivy-clad ruins in the churchyard at Ilsington and with the carved granite stones which lie around the village, some built into hedges and walls, others in the walls of houses, and others discarded in odd corners, and rubbish tips, or at least they were until I came along. What desecration took place in the 1870s when the ancient Manor House of Ilsington was finally demolished and these skilfully carved and moulded stones were deliberately smashed into pieces for the building of the walls of the new wing of the Old Vicarage, the coachman's house and outbuildings (now the Post Office), the wall to the Vicarage Kitchen Garden, all for the Rev. Robert Lovett and, a few years later in 1873, for the school and school-house and the walls of the new School Road.

These moulded stones were the mullions and arches of the mansion's windows and doors, and two of them which have come to light within the past two years have letters and numbers on them. One in Town Barton courtyard has what appears to be the letter R and underneath number 1 and what may be a 6. The other at the Ilsington Post Office has a letter B, and underneath a 4. If these two stones are the smashed remains of a single stone (tantalizingly the middle bit is missing), what can these letters mean? I have looked at the names of those connected with George Ford who supposedly rebuilt or added to the Manor House about 1550 but there are no clues.

In vain I have searched for a drawing or a print of the old mansion but again I have drawn a blank. Some time ago however I came across this description of it published in *Trewman's Exeter Flying Post* in August 1851.

The remains of a mouldering mansion house, once vast and venerable, form a very pleasing object from the precinct of Ilsington Church. Unfortunately a great portion has been taken down and what remains, although picturesque enough, forms a confused mass of old architectural outlines, which require some difficulty to assign, if not to period, at least to anything like symmetry and the original organisation. The conviction of a manorial dwelling however flashes there on the vision, and the tourist cannot but muse and ponder on the dim prestige of an old house, mullioned and bracketed (corbelled) and embayed all over, though all that is now left is a mere skeleton phantom of the past and of days of wassail, war, emnity, love and revelry. There are traces of a quadrangle, of an arch which connected it with a second, and the mullions, now masoned up, of the old windows in the kitchen and out offices are still traceable in ruined conditions, in once busy abodes, turned now into cow-houses and repositories for farming gear and waste matters of all varieties. The elegant porch which formed the entrance also exists, and the sites of various halls and chambers and fireplaces are still traceable. Years back the house was inhabited by divers families, till it became in too tottering a state for the safety of the inmates. About 1635 when the fines and prosecutions of the infamous Star Chamber flourished at their height, enactments were made to compel the country gentlemen to reside more on their estates, instead of idling their time amid the festivities of the metropolis. During the time of James II many old houses were abandoned however to 'the moles and the bats' and consequently degenerated into farms and cottages, the possessors preferring the court gaieties to rural distant and solitary pursuits.

Some years ago when the heaps of rubble from the site of the Old Vicarage were being removed and dumped at Rixeypark, Chudleigh, to be used as hardcore, I noticed some of these carved stones among the rubble. I bought four or five lorry-loads of the rubble and was lucky enough to save about a dozen of these carved stones. But how many of these precious stones were buried, never to be seen again?

I suspect that some of these stones also were taken for the rebuilding of Ingsdon Manor House. The ruins of the Ilsington Manor House were owned by Capt. C.J.H. Monro of Ingsdon. I believe the two main gate posts of Ingsdon have them in their construction.

Bagtor Mill in the early 1900s. The Manor mill of Bagtor was controlled by the Lord of the Manor who collected dues from his tenants for milling corn ground in his manor. The vicar of Ilsington too required his tithes from the miller.

14 - Settlements, Hamlets and Farms

Every farm in Ilsington parish has existed at least since the 13th or 14th century: seven hundred years or 28 generations of farmers are bound to have accumulated some interesting history, but the pity of it is that much of it has been lost for ever. Intimate stories of all those people, their happiness and sorrow, their fortunes and losses, are all unknown to us; yet they knew the same hills and valleys, the same tors and streams, the same old grey church on the hill, as we do. Haytor Rock in all its weathers was as familiar to them as it is to us. They faced many of their houses towards the dip in the hills to the east, where they could see the sea, but in those early days few of them ever ventured the twelve miles to stand by it.

In many cases we do know the names of those old parishioners, recorded as a stark entry in the baptism, marriage and burial entries in the church registers and, where old deeds and documents of a farm still exist and are available to be studied, a little more can be found out. Perhaps a marriage settlement will disclose a bride's dowry, a conveyance will reveal some history of the land, or a will may uncover the ultimate possessions of the yeoman farmer, his cattle, his chattels.

Many such documents lie today in some solicitor's storeroom, or in a farm attic mouldering and unlooked at, for they are not needed in modern conveyancing and many have already been burnt or made into lamp-shades. A few years ago I was lucky to save a few documents referring to land which had been purchased about a hundred and fifty years ago by the late Alfred Lyon of Middlecott, and so a little of the history of Smallacombe Farm is known today whereas it would have been lost for ever.

It is almost unbelievable, but a fact, that the number of working farms in the parish of Ilsington at the time of writing is only 11, whereas going back 160 years to the year 1839 at the time of the tithe survey there were 53, and to 1878, during the Depression, it had halved to 23. From then until ten years ago the number kept fairly stable, but since then it has fallen dramatically. Of the 11 today, only two do any milking – Robert Hendy's Colesworthy, and Raymond Beard's Coombe.

From early times there were two farms in Ilsington Village, one the demesne or home farm of the manor called Court Barton and the other let on lease called Town Farm, or Town Barton, or Shears Tenement. Being so close together, their fields were intermingled but generally those of Town Barton were west of the village and Court Barton to the east. Probably the farmhouse of the latter was the present Carpenters Arms, and the former stood on the site of the present farmhouse but was an ancient thatched longhouse building.

Farming was one of the original industries of the parish. In early times the first farms had existed on the higher moorland but, as the weather deteriorated over the centuries, these were gradually abandoned and the valleys and lower land became cultivated. Throughout the country the Black Death caused a large decrease in population during the 14 century, with land becoming uncultivated and unfarmed by late Tudor times.

At the lower end of the parish was a huge heath joining the neighbouring heaths in the parishes of Bovey Tracey, Teigngrace, Hennock, Kingsteignton and Highweek. This heath was very marshy and boggy, and all roads and tracks skirted it.

Between the moorland and this heathland farmers found some very fertile ground and a considerable number of animals were reared and crops grown. But the tops of the hills were generally left uncultivated, as were the steep slopes, and largely remained so until the late 18th century and later.

Writing in 1808 the historian Charles Vancouver states that a large proportion of the land was in the hands of the yeomanry or owner occupiers whereas in the past it had been leased on terms of 99 years determinable on 3 lives – a most unsatisfactory way of holding and farming land. He says most of the farmhouses are in sheltered valleys but this meant dung for fertilising the fields had to be carried uphill on horseback.

Vancouver comments that the common Devonshire plough made by a hedgerow carpenter seldom costs more than 15/-. It was pulled by 2 horses or a strong pair of steers but when an old ley was ploughed a double or sometimes treble force was required.

GROWING AND HARVESTING CORN

This is so different today to what it was like back in the 1930 and 1940s. In those days the field was ploughed, rolled and worked well with harrows, or drags as they were called locally, in several directions by horses or early tractors until the soil was pliant and you could bury the toe of your boot easily in any direction.

Then the seed was tilled, here at Narracombe by a corn drill which needed a man riding on the drill to see that the spout did not become choked. Meanwhile the seed was dressed against wireworm, preferably turning it over with a shovel on the barn floor but more often in the drill, by throwing some dressing over the corn and turning it over with your hands. (The dressing was said to be highly poisonous on the label but who believed it!).

The drill was originally pulled by 2 horses but later converted to tractor use. The method was to go around the field clockwise 4 or 5 times, giving a wide forrard for turning, and then up and down working across the field. When it was all tilled it was usually rolled again (unless it was winter corn which would weather during the winter – or if grass seeds were being sown), and left.

Weeds, especially charlock, would grow and in the early days up to the 1920s such weeds would have been hoed out by manual labour, but later left or lightly harrowed, until it was considered fit to cut, usually 6 weeks after coming into ear.

If the crop was oats it was cut by a self-binder (2 horses or a tractor) which cut the corn, collected it into sheaves and bound and tied each sheaf with a strand of binder cord. The sheaves were tossed out on the ground and had to be manually picked up, one under each arm and stood up in stitches or stooks (for oats 6 sheaves to a stitch). This was achieved by ramming the butts of the sheaves on the ground and at the same time pushing the tops together.

Oats had to stand 10 days in the field (said to 'hear the church bells twice') to finish ripening, before being carried to the rick. The stitches must not fall down during that time or they would have to be re-stitched for the corn itself would sprout if it touched wet earth.

There were many other difficulties at this time. If the weather was continuously wet the sheaves would have to be turned within their ties to get the insides to dry. If the corn started to sprout then as a last resort the cord ties would have to be cut and the sheaves carried to the rick loose.

Another difficulty was that the sheaves often contained many thistles (I have known 75% thistles and 25% straw), and they had to be stood up in the some way – remember it was not done in those days to wear gloves when farming, except occasionally for hedging.

If everything went well, oats could be harvested from the stitches at 10 days, and carried to the rickyard. Here ricks were built on a bed of faggots of wood, tops of bushes and trees bound in neat bundles, 3 feet long 1 foot deep, the tops laid in alternate ways and trimmed, bound with a whippy hazel stick twisted together at the end to form a knot. Brouse or hedge parings were laid on top of the faggots, the whole to form a slightly oval bed seven paces long and five paces wide.

The rick was built by the rickmaker on his knees, taking 2 sheaves at a time and going around the rick clockwise putting one sheaf partly under the other. He worked around and around like this covering the butt of one round with the tie of the previous round, until he reached the middle. It was important to keep the middle filled up so that if any dampness got in it would drain to the outside.

TITHE SURVEY 1839–1840

The Tithe Survey records the number of farms and holdings in Ilsington in 1840, just over 150 years or 2 lifetimes ago. Another document, the Parish Rates of 1856 (see opposite), also provides details of the size of farms, the owners and occupiers in the middle of the 19th century. This makes interesting reading when compared to the state of farming and the countryside today.

Of course, the subject of farming in Ilsington parish is a vast one. Indeed there is more than enough material in the author's hands to complete a book on Narracombe Farm alone. However, for the purposes of *The Book of Ilsington* selective farms and holdings are looked at in turn in order to provide an overview of farms and farming in the parish.

1856 PARISH RATES

	A R P	OWNERS	OCCUPIERS
Glebe house + land	4-2-9	Dean of Windsor	T. Atkinson
Town	53-3-2	C H Munro	Richard Stranger
Court	15-1-7	C H Munro	-do-
Glebe	81-2-26	Rev. C. Marsham	John Rowell
North Sigford	76-1-5	Chas Wills	Chas Wills
Honeywell	109-0-0	Wm Lambshead	Wm Lambshead
Honeywell Down	18-1-9	Samuel Lambshead	Samuel Lambshead
Pinchaford	7-1-11	Samuel Lambshead	-do-
Kennypark Well	17-3-33	William Hatherley	Samuel Southey
Hindsground	21-3-33	Chas Wills	Wm Lambshead
Pinchaford	132-2-30	W White	John Lambshead
Kennypark Well	3-2-13	William Hatherley	Samuel Bailey
Rowells	16-1-3	G Templer	John Sowton
Smallacombe	167-0-19	Joseph Wills	Joseph Wills
Oldatown	36-3-0	John Kingwill	Mark Northcott
Middlecott	66-3-4	John Rowell	John Rowell
Puddicombe	21-3-2	Alexander Adair	Geo. Hellier
Narracombe	144-0-9	Geo Wills	Geo Wills
Brimley	74-3-8	Geo Wills	-do-
Brimley	3-2-7	John Mann	Mary Holmes
Woodhouse	75-0-37	Wm Mortimore	Wm Mortimore
Lenda	64-0-25	Geo G Wills	Wm Wills
Bagtor Barton	670-1-36	Lord Cranstown	Rd & Hy Irish
Bagtor Mill	12-0-84	-do-	John Tickle
Westerbrook	46-1-13	-do-	Joseph Winsor
Emsworthy	81-1-17	-do-	Rd & Hy Irish
East Horridge	210-1-19	Richard Kingwill	Nicholas Moalle
West Horridge	221-0-7	James Woodley	John Moalle
Mountsland	88-1-23	Thos Rowell	John Easterbrook
Pt Mountsland	25-3-12	Richard Rowell	Richard Rowell
Pt Mountsland	24-1-12	Wm Kingwill	James Vallance
Cross Parks	6-0-12	Thos Widger	Thos Cleave
Lower Sigford	97-2-38	Samuel Widger	Samuel Widger
Lower Sigford	86-3-15	Samuel Widger	Thos Widger

	A R P	OWNERS	OCCUPIERS
Lower Sigford	83-0-12	Berry	Joshua Berry
Crownley Park	24-1-14	?	Joshua Berry
Higher Sigford	150-2-16	James Woodley	Hy John Clark
Coombe & Claws	56-2-20	Samuel Lambshead	Samuel Lambshead
Beffield & Bridgeland	24-0-33	Samuel Lambshead	-do-
East Lounston	95-2-26	Thos Shapter	Geo Rowell
Higher Lounston	99-0-4	James Wills	Wm Rowell
Great Lounston	120-2-30	Stephen Nosworthy	John & Geo Wills
Lower Lounston	63-8-10	Wm Langley	John Reeves
Custreet	41-1-8	C H Monro	Wm Rowell
Hill	49-2-20	Jonas Mitchell	Jonas Mitchell
Liverton	66-3-55	James Woodley	-do-
Pool and Wills	50-3-20	Wm Widger	Wm Widger
Halford	52-0-8	Candy Trustees	Stephen Kingwill
Belle View	30-3-32	John Divett	Thos Rowell
Halford	28-0-0	Francis Rowell	Tuckett
Willsworthy	64-0-0	John Divett	-do-
Colesworthy (part of)	123-3-6	Duke of Somerset	Jonas Mitchell
Rora	191-0-0	Lewis Filmore	Wm Mortimore
Stancombe	112-3-3	Rev Chas Wolston	John Harris
Coldeast	16-3-36	Francis Rowell	Tuckett
Great Colesworthy	133-3-30	John Rowell	John Rowell
Yonder Colesworthy	135-3-37	John Divett	Thos Elliott
Shuteparks	5-3-38	Lord Graves	John Hayman
Liverton Mill	8-3-1	Chas. Wills	Geo Mortimore
Staplehill	102-0-1	Duke of Somerset	John Rowell
Ingsdon	336-1-35	C H Monro	C H Monro
Knighton	83-0-2	Henry Bickford	John Steve
Knighton	-	Ann Harris	Ann Harris
Knighton	40-1-35	Rev Geo Smith	Joseph Mann jun
Lower Millands	12-3-37	Wm Thorn	Wm Thorn
Higher Millands	26-1-17	Thos Rowell	Thos Rowell
Ingsdon Mill	3-0-30	Richard Thorn	Wm Thorn
Olditch	10-3-33	Joseph Rowell	Joseph Mann jun

Note ARP = acres, roods and perches

• BAGTOR •

The Domesday Book records that Ordric was in possession of Bagtor before the Norman conquest, and that after it was granted to Nicholas, chief balister, with Roger de Augville as tenant. Passing through the de Baggetorre family it came to the Beares and to the Fords of Chagford and Ashburton. From the Fords it descended through marriage to the Stawells and Drakes to Thomas Tothill and remained in that family until it was sold to John Dunning, Lord Ashburton, and passed to the Lord Cranstown by marriage. Since that time it has had several owners including the Whitley family who had the manor house thatched, Mrs Perrim an American who purchased the dilapidated building for under £1000 in about 1960, and (in 1997) Nigel and Susan Sawrey-Cookson the present owners who have completely renovated the Elizabethan part of the house.

Above: *Bagtor Manor House c.1900. The Queen Anne hipped-roof front was built on to the Elizabethan house in the 1770s (fifty years or so after the fashion had ceased in London), very likely after John Dunning, Lord Ashburton, had purchased it.*

Left: *Bagtor House c.1925.*

Left: *Cottages at Millcombe, Bagtor Mill. Originally there were five dwellings here and, more recently, two. There is now one, Lemon Cottage, until recently the home of Lord and Lady Tebbit.*

Below: *The overshot wheel at Bagtor Mill. It was manufactured by Henry Beare's iron foundry at Liverton. The mill leat carrying water to turn the wheel came from the River Sig. This was the manor mill of Bagtor and was owned with the manor until the 1950s. Tenants included the Tarr, Hayman, Tickle families, and Samuel Giles.*

Bottom: *Boundary stone between Saddle Tor and Haytor marked 'B' and 'I' to denote the boundary between Bagtor and Ilsington manors.*

Below: *Mrs Fernley Collins standing at her door at Bagtor Mill Cottage. This is one of a row of five original cottages built for workers at Bagtor Manor. In the background is Birchanger Ball, open moorland, now planted. The lane ran at the back of the cottages and it was possible, when the author's father, Sydney Wills, went to school in the 1880s, for the boys to run up over the thatched roof and put a hessian sack on the chimney, smoking out the cottagers!*

Bagtor Barton, the demesne or home farm of Bagtor Manor. It was owned with the Manor until sold by Herbert Whitley to Harold Retallick about 1975. Tenants under the Manor included the Veal, Irish, Smerdon, Mortimore and Fowler families. Now owned by Maurice and Pauline Retallick. It is one of the few farm long-houses left in the parish. Note the wooden granary with its thatched roof built on staddle stones to the right.

• BRIMLEY •

BRIMLEY (LANGALLER)

The manor of Brimley is unusual in that it lies in two parishes, that of Ilsington and Bovey Tracey. As long ago as 1602 there was a dispute where the tenants of the manor should take their corn to be ground: Bovey Mill claiming that it should be taken there so that they could collect the dues.

The author is of the opinion that the origin of this settlement goes back to Domesday times when fifteen thanes are mentioned as holding lands attached to Bovey Manor, one of these holding Pullabrook. Later it was given to Edmund Tudor on his creation as Earl of Richmond by King Henry VI his half-brother, in 1453, thus gaining the name of 'Richmond's Lands'. At his death in 1457 they would have passed to his widow formerly Margaret Beaufort, and from her to Edmund and Margaret's son, later King Henry VII, becoming Crown Lands, thus giving rise to the tradition that Yarner was once a royal hunting lodge. Ancient deeds show they remained Crown Lands during the reigns of Henry VII, Henry VIII and Edward VI but they were sold piecemeal to the tenants, who bought their holdings with high interest mortgages. It is possible too that this area was sometime connected to a priory in Monmouthshire and the Knights of St John of Jerusalem.

The author has photocopies of the court rolls of the manor from 1602 which he acquired from the Devon Record Office many years ago. It was possible to read those from the 18th century but the earlier ones were written in abbreviated Latin script and for a long time no one could be found to decipher it. Eventually Valerie Ransom translated them. At the time she was investigating some boxes of deeds at Ullacombe, and the two were connected; Ullacombe also being part of these ancient lands.

The annual court of the manor of Brimley or Langaller was held at Lower Brimley when the tenants and freeholders were summoned to attend and pay fealty to the steward of the lord of the manor. Any infringement of rights were presented to the court and those found guilty were fined or amerced. Thus in 1728 one of my ancestors, Richard Leare of Narracombe, was presented 'for not attending upon the jury in spite of a warning being left at his house' and in 1736 his son Thomas, was fined a shilling for not attending court to take the office of tithingman.

New tenants and freeholders had to attend court to be sworn in, and looking through the court rolls the descent of the different properties can be traced. The records point to an early break-up of the manor into small estates.

Higher Brimley from Leys Field in 1995. A new field, Boodown Gratna, and a lone oak stand on the horizon.

HIGHER BRIMLEY

The hamlet of Higher Brimley is officially all in Ilsington parish and Lower Brimley is the part in Bovey Tracey parish, a fact not recognised today by the postal authorities or by many people living in the area. At the break-up of the manor of Brimley, Higher Brimley became four farms and by the beginning of the 19th century had dwindled to two: one owned by George Wills (1778–1815) on the higher side of the road, anciently owned by the Furlongs and Corbyns, and the other on the lower side farmed by William Mardon. The latter had the ancient Hall House as its farmhouse. In 1834 the author's great-grandfather came of age and inherited the former, and purchased Mardon's, and both were added to Narracombe. In the 1860s the Hall House was demolished to build Brimley Barn, which in turn was converted into a house to again become a dwelling, 'Summer Meadow'.

In dozens of parchment deeds we have the intricate descent of the fields of the former farms which can be traced over 300 years. Many of the old buildings shown in the 1839 tithe map have long since disappeared and Higher Brimley has changed from being a self-contained community of over fifty people with its own bake-house, shop, its own dressmakers, serge-weavers, carpenters, masons, copper and tin miners, thatchers and many other crafts (and even, in 1871, a Greenwich Out-Pensioner), to the small quiet hamlet of today.

The well building Higher Brimley Farm. Until mains water came to Higher Brimley in 1923 there was little water in the hamlet. Schemes had been made through the centuries to bring water from the Doxwell spring by an underground culvert, and by sinking wells. Brimley Farm was supplied by two stone-built tanks (one shown here) with rainwater from the roofs.

Clockwise from top left: 1. Higher Brimley Farmhouse (now Corbyn's Brimley) and its fields, now all part of Narracombe. Higher Brimley and Narracombe were joined in 1808 with the marriage of the author's great-great-grandparents, George Wills (1778–1815) and Mary Nosworthy (1778–1827). 2. Frank Wills, with Higher Brimley in the background, 1925. 3. The disintegrating ruins of Mardon's Farm cattle sheds built of cob and stone with a thatched roof, as seen from the Leys Field side. It was demolished in 1972. Mardon's farm was bought in 1845 by my great-grandfather George Wills of Narracombe (1813–1893) and added to Narracombe. 4. Brimley Barn at Higher Brimley before being converted into 'Summer Meadow' in 1972. The barn was built by George Wills of Narracombe in the 1850s–60s, erected on the site of Mardon's farmhouse which, in the 17th century, had been the 'Hall House' of Higher Brimley.

• CANDY FARM •

Candy Farm lay close to the hamlet of Halford near Liverton. It is reputed that William Candy, a travelling musician, settled at this farm, then called Hore's Tenement, about 1715, and farmed it until his death in 1727. He then bequeathed it to the parish for the relief of the parish poor.

Since then it has been owned by his trustees and let to numerous tenants.

Profits from the farm have been paid out by providing Candy coats and Christmas gifts to the old and needy, and special gifts to parishioners at difficult times.

• COLESWORTHY •

No doubt Colesworthy (Colsway) was originally a Saxon settlement and by the early 13th century was known as Caulesweye. In 1299 an inquisition post mortem held on the death of Oliver Dinham, lord of the manor of Ilsington, mentions that there are mills on the property. In the middle of the 13th century Michael De Cauliswey is mentioned as Dinham's tenant. By 1542 Colesworthy seems to have been divided into two holdings and few years later Hugh Pomeroy of Ingsdon bought both of them. His daughter Margaret married James Woodley of Halshanger and the property is then described as 'Lands in Chettisbeare (deep wooded valley among hills) and Cawleswaye.' The Woodleys seem to have considered it a minor manor, the centre of considerable acreage around Liverton some which they owned up to the middle of the 19th century. They sold the capital messuage, barton farm and demesne lands of Colesway to Robert Bearne of Newton Bushell in 1773 and in the Land Tax Returns John Rowell is said to be owner of 'Great Colesworthy' in 1780. Since then it has been owned by the Divetts, Church Commissioners, E. Chugg and now John and Margaret Hendy, and their son Robert, with the Cleaves as tenants for several years in the 19th century.

Now one of the two farms in the parish to produce milk. The smaller farm of Yonder Colesworthy was owned and farmed by John Paddon in 1780 who sold to Branscombe about 1840, Richard Wills farmed it in 1841, and the Elliott family until sold to the Divetts, when it was joined to Great Colesworthy.

• COMBE FARM •

Combe Farm is situated on the Bickington boundary of the parish near Ramshorn Down in the manor of Sigford. It held rights on Ramshorn Down until a field called Bridgeland, 4.9, acres was purchased in 1817, adjoining Rora, and with it came common rights within the Manor of Ilsington on Haytor Down.

In 1630 it is mentioned in the Ilsington Church Rate the owners being John Gifford and William Luscombe, and in a Narracombe deed of 1637 when a settlement of lands in Higher Brimley by John Bowdon the elder of Coombe is mentioned

Earlier there are mentions in the church registers when children of John Gifford de Combe are baptized in 1617 and 1619 and two generations of John Gifford's are buried in 1612 and 1666.

In 1780 it was owned by a John Wills and let to John Cator and later to George Mortimore. In 1810 the owner was Jacob Wills and tenant James Sanders. In 1835 Samuel Lambshead, Jacob Wills' son-in-law, was owner of the 56 acres. It was then called Coombe and Claws.

Sometime about 1880 the farmhouse was burnt down and rooms were made as a temporary dwelling above the shippens. Later tenants/owners were George Reeves, Monty Lear and Jack Bowden. It was then purchased by Raymond Beard who still farms it. It is at the time of writing one of the two farms in the parish which produces milk.

• COURT BARTON •

Court Barton, or the Barton of Ilsington, was the home farm of the manor house of Ilsington, sometimes called The Manor Place, Court, the Mansion House.

The most ancient farm in the parish, it must have been farmed since there was a manor at this spot, but all traces of the early farmhouse and buildings of wood, cob and thatch would be gone and built-over several times. The present structure of the Carpenters Arms (16th century) is thought to have been the farmhouse until c.1815 when it became a public house, replacing the Church House Inn (No.3 St Michael's Cottages).

The Farmhouse then moved to the semi-derelict mansion house at the top of the hill, until it became so ruinous that it was abandoned about 1830.

Belonging to the owners of Ingsdon for many years, it was farmed by James Mudge in 1780 and by Robert Pethybridge in 1805. Charles Corbyn Wills of Town Barton had the lease in 1810 and farmed the land until he sold Town Barton to the Hale-Monros of Ingsdon in 1844, thus joining the two farms.

The only two buildings, except the Carpenters Arms, belonging to the Court Barton today are the

Pigeon or Culver Cottage, the residence of Mr and Mrs John Smith, and the old barn opposite the Carpenters Arms, now converted into a house by Mr and Mrs Bill Edwards.

Pigeon Cottage has number of pigeon holes in the gable ends of the main roof, enabling the occupants of the old manor to have a source of fresh meat at any time of the year as required.

• COXLAND •

Coxland, formerly Cockslen, and mentioned in the 1332 Assize Rolls as Cockesland, is a smallholding in the Manor of Sigford. The fields are now part of Higher Sigford Farm. It is mentioned in 1530 as owned by John Coplestone of Yealmpton, in the 1630 Ilsington Church Rate assessment by Ffrysewyde Bowden, and in the 1641 will of John Lambshead. In 1780 it was owned by the Rev Peter Woodley of Halshanger and let to John Rowell, 28 acres.

It is thought that the old farmhouse was burnt down in 18th century and the land joined to Higher Sigford. It was later sold by the Woodleys to the Mortimore family. In 1725 the Rowells occupied it. The house is now owned by Mr and Mrs Heasell.

• CROWNLEY •

Crownley, known previously as Crastland and Croundell is a smallholding on the River Lemon above Bagtor Mill. It was once part of the Bagtor estate, but in the Manor of Ilsington, and is mentioned in the 1566 survey of Ilsington Manor where George Ford 'holds certain lands in Crastland in free socage and pays one pair of white spurs annually.' In 1685 it was sold by the Manor to Gunston (see also Hindsground).

In 1748, having been separated from the Manor, Thomas Rowell of Ilsington sold the one moiety of the property to Nicholas Tarr of Ilsington, miller, mentioning that it had already passed through several hands.

The old farmhouse at Crownley which farmed thirty acres of land. Further up the valley on the moor tin was mined for many years at Crownley Works.

• CUSTREET - GORSE BLOSSOM •

There are numerous references to this holding in the parish records. It is an ancient farm of the Manor of Ingsdon adjoining Ilsington Heathfield. It is mentioned in the 1306 assizes as Corryngestrete. Thomas Mayior paid its church rate in 1630. By 1780 it had been sold from the manor and owned by the Bailey family and let to John Rowell, and later the Mann family. In 1856 its 41 acres had been repurchased by C. H. Monro of Ingsdon and remained in that family until bought by Miss Mollie Mann, later Mrs Warne when it was renamed Gorse Blossom farm. Now it has ceased to be a farm and is run as a model railway by G. Kitchenside.

• EMSWORTHY •

Emsworthy, or Emsery, was an early smallholding sited on the moor in the valley of the Beckabrook below Saddle Tor. It was part of the Manor of Bagtor and leased by Thomas Tothill of Bagtor in 1714 to Richard Bayley with the proviso that he rebuild the house, cow house, barn and wood house within two years. Tenanted by William Winsor in 1820, and Michael Cumming in 1910, the house is said to have been destroyed by fire. Now only a barn remains and is part of Holwell.

• FURSMANS •

This very old farmhouse at South Knighton was farmed anciently by the Fursland family. In 1780 it was owned and farmed by John Motton, and later by the Harris family who let to the Rowells, Pennys and Johns.

• GREEN LANE •

The building of Green Lane started in 1921 when the author's father, Sydney Wills, bought an old army hut and put it in the corner of a Narracombe field called Higher Clampitts for letting as a holiday chalet. It was 1921 and it was only just possible to do such a thing for the mains water had just come to the area, with a new main from Haytor to Brimley.

My father named the chalet Green Lane Bungalow because the lane from there to the Bovey Road was always green in the middle, and the junction at the top was known as Green Lane End from where the path continued across the moor to meet the Manaton road. Little did he know that Narracombe, or Woodhouse Lane as it was then called, was an ancient trackway, a pre-

The first bungalow to be built at Green Lane was an ex-army hut from the Great War. It was placed in the corner of Higher Clampitts field in 1921. Let as a holiday chalet for several years, it was sold in 1929.

historic ridge road, later to be given the name 'green lanes', or that the lane formed the boundary between Ilsington and Langaller manors.

Gradually my father sold off pieces of land during the difficult days of farming in the late 1920s and early 30s. Runswick followed Green Lane Bungalow, then a succession of dwellings were built, right up to the 1970s. In all this building Narracombe had lost a shelter copse with three fields (including its so-called largest field, Forty Acres, which turned out to be a fraud as it was only one acre!).

An aerial view of Green Lane taken in 1972. The dwellings shown in the photograph and dates of construction (where known) include: Journey's End (1930), Green Lane Bungalow (1921), By-the-Way (1937), Runswick (1923), Mooracre (1948), Outalong (1927), Brae Birnie (1925), Crow's Nest (1950), Wimstone (1952), The Cleft (1938), Byloes (1951), Grey Gables (1936), Windycroft (1929), Pitstone (1970), Moorgate (1932), The Patch (1937), Tetherstone (1934), Lewside (1955).

• HALFORD •

Halford or Hartford is one of the ancient hamlets of Ilsington parish, containing a cluster of small farms and cottages. It is situated on the edge of Ilsington Heathfield where villagers had the right to graze their geese and to pick black-sticks for kindling their fires and hearths ('blacksticks' being the remains of gorse after it has been swaled, or burnt).

Candy Farm was one of the Halford farms, farmed by William Candy (see Candy Farm) whose charitable bequest is mention elsewhere in this book.

Cottages at Halford, probably dating from the 16th or 17th centuries. The left-hand building was once a farm-house. The hamlet bordered on the vast Ilsington Heathfield on which, following its enclosure in 1809 the villagers lost their right to graze cattle, sheep, ponies and geese, and the right to gather peat, furze, and kindling wood for their fires.

• HAYTOR VALE •

The small village of Haytor Vale nestles within the shadow of Haytor Rock and the moor. It was largely built by George Templer of Stover to house the quarrymen working nearby. He also built the Rock Inn in their midst. At the top and bottom of the Vale (at Ludgate and Cottamoor) he erected iron gates, thus making a private enclave in which local people were not welcomed, There are now twelve cottages, the Post Office and the Inn in the Vale and one of the first tasks of the Parish Council when it was formed in 1894 was to make the road a public highway. Mains water was laid on in 1914 and the construction of other dwellings followed.

A photograph taken c.1910 from the Rock Inn. Note that the road was then a sandy path. It had remained a private road until the 1900s.

HAYTOR VALE IN 1881

Just over a hundred years ago there were no houses at Haytor except the present cottages of Haytor Vale with the Rock Inn in the middle of them. No Ludgate, no Moorland Hotel, no houses along Gold Flake Lane, no houses down the Ilsington road until you reached the two cottages beside the road, now called Heather Cottage and Bracken Tor, except of course the ancient farmstead of Pinchaford with several cottages in the valley.

Haytor Vale as it was then just beginning to be called (it was known as Haytor Buildings before), consisted of 19 back-to-back cottages and a pub, all of which George Templer had built for his quarry workers some sixty years before. In 1881 there were 83 inhabitants, 47 males and 36 females; their ages averaged 28 years and 32 years respectively. Fifty-eight had been born within the parish of Ilsington, twelve elsewhere in Devon, nine in Cornwall, three in Somerset and one in Wales. The oldest women were Sarah Bailey, aged 85, who was born at Highweek, and Mary Campion, 79, born at Modbury, and the oldest men Samuel Bailey, 85, born at Highweek, and William Hawkes, 80, born in Ilsington. His baptism is recorded in the Ilsington Church Registers July 5th 1801, William son of John and Jane Hawkes. Samuel and Sarah Bailey were the parents of Sarah Hicks, whose name is still remembered in Haytor Vale as being one of the last of the old Dame School teachers, and her husband Thomas Hicks had a smallholding of ten acres in the village.

Then came James Taylor, a journeyman blacksmith, whose two sons George (aged 16) and Edwin (14) were already described as iron miners, and next door John Northcott (24) another iron-miner and his young family. Then came William Hawkes (80) still described as a labourer and his wife, with their lodger Thomas Johns a carpenter from St Germans. Richard Allen (50) an iron miner from Callington and his Dittisham born wife lived next door, and then Charles Cocks (70) and his wife Temperance and unmarried children Mary (39), a dressmaker, and Charles (28) a labourer and grandson aged 15. Another son, William Cocks, an iron-miner lived next door with his wife Lydia and four children, and then Samuel Taylor (64), his wife Mary, and grandchildren George Wellington (18) and Ernest Wellington (13) already described as a farm labourer.

Lewis Campion (38) was the landlord at the Rock Inn and Sarah his wife, née Taylor. They had two children, Marion and Lewis, and two lodgers both iron-miners. Then came George Taylor (34) a carpenter and his Cornish born wife and children, and John Wellington (49) an iron-miner born in Cornwall, his Ilsington born wife and two children Mabel and Leah. Elizabeth Winsor (77) widow of Jacob Winsor lived by herself, and then came the Jenkin family: Richard (25) was an iron-miner born in Cornwall, his wife born at St Blazey, and baby daughter born in Wales. They shared part of a cottage with copper-miner James Boyler (25), his wife and baby son all born in Somerset, and a Cornish iron-miner James Giles (24). Next came the Beer family from Meshaw and Morchard Bishop, another iron-miner, followed by another family of Northcotts, the father William (49) a farm labourer, daughter Mary a dressmaker, and their sons an iron-miner and farm labourer. At No. 16 Mary

Campion (79) and her unmarried son an iron-miner lived, and next door Joseph Osborn (45) another iron-miner and his wife Mahala. Then came Frederick Brimicombe (48), iron-miner, born in Ilsington, his wife Charlotte, and son Charles, and a lodger born at Constantine an iron-miner. In the last house at the end of the village the Stancombe family, James (32) iron-miner, Sarah, and four children. The Vale must have been a very different place to what it is like today, and I have always heard it said that many parishioners would not pass that way at night. Actually the road from Ludgate to Cottamoor (or Two Posts as it used to be called) was a private road, which belonged to the Lord of the Manor, as all the houses in the Vale did.

HAYTOR VALE

Haytor Vale, 1948. The Post Office was then in the end cottage kept by Jack and Emily Morrish.

Haytor Vale, or 'the Buildings' as they used to be called, seen from the field opposite on which the annual Haytor sheep sale was held.

The building of Haytor Vale began in the 1820s although a smallholding, Kennapark Well, existed here before that date. In the late nineteenth century private dwellings began to appear. Here is 'Firtrees', 'The Pines' (once a Post Office), and 'Woodlands' to the right.

The first private house to be built in Haytor Vale was the property of George Taylor, about 1880.

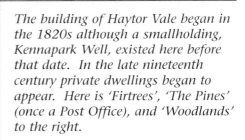

HAYTOR VALE

View of the Oldertown, Shotts area (c. 1940) and houses built on land owned by the Lyon family of Middlecott, and designed by architect Thomas Henry Lyon. The land, formerly part of Oldertown Farm is mentioned in the 1566 survey of Ilsington Manor as 'divers parcels of land called Lez Shotts lying in common', suggesting it was still common land.

The Shotts, Haytor. The round building on the right was the powder house for the adjoining iron mines where gunpowder kept for blasting was stored. The Shotts was built on an old mine track running from Green Lane End to the iron mine adit and works. Later other houses were built on this track, including Bel Alp which became Violet Wills' estate between 1923 and 1950. Locals called it 'Gold Flake Lane' after Dame Violet's connection with the W.D. & H.O. Wills tobacco company.

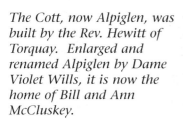

The Cott, now Alpiglen, was built by the Rev. Hewitt of Torquay. Enlarged and renamed Alpiglen by Dame Violet Wills, it is now the home of Bill and Ann McCluskey.

• HINDSGROUND •

The fact that there are remains of a Bronze Age hut circle existing in one of the copses of Hindsground, the land on the west bank of the River Lemon adjoining Pinchaford Ball, shows that the land has been settled and cultivated for about 3000 years. Probably however the area was not enclosed with the walls and hedges of today, until after the neighbouring lands of Pinchaford and Crownley (see separate section on Crownley), and that the moorland of Pinchaford Ball then joined the much later enclosed lands of Stapledon, Honeywell Down and Birchanger Ball. When it was enclosed, two tongues of common land on either side of the enclosed part, extending to the public highway, were left for access to Pinchaford Ball; hence the two lanes of today.

The first written reference to Hindsground is contained in the 1566 Survey of Ilsington Manor being 'an inquiry held on Saturday, the 17th August in the eighth year of the reign of Queen Elizabeth on behalf of the share of Henry Compton, esquire, one of the Lords of the Manor of Ilsington.' In this Hindsground is mentioned by its ancient name of Crastland and it says 'George Ford holds certain lands in Crastland in free socage (a feudal tenure involving payment of rent or other service) with two suits of court, and he pays per annum one pair of white spurs'.

The boundaries of the Manorial Waste or Common are also described and here again there is reference to this land, 'From Prowses Mead End (somewhere near the Moorland Hotel) the boundary goes south by a wall or an old ditch towards Crondell (Crownley) unto the lands of George Ford called Croftlondes or Crastlondes, and from thence by the south side of Bynchen Ball (Pinchaford Ball) turning over in the midst of Smallamoor, westwards almost to Lether Tor (Saddle Tor) and thence north to a river.'

From George Ford the land passed down to his descendant Edward Holwell Drake who sold it to my great-great-great-grandfather Charles Wills of Town Barton in 1774. His mother had been the last of the old Corbyn family of Ilsington, who through the years had amassed a small fortune in land. When Charles died in 1791 his eldest son

Charles Corbyn Wills, or 'King Charlie' as he was nick-named, inherited the property. In the 1838 Tithe Survey he is named as owning the 21 acres 3 roods 33 perches of Hindsground with John Hannaford as tenant. He may have been the original hind of Hindsground.

In 1858 Hindsground, then described as Hines or Barn or Croftland, was sold by C. C. Wills jnr. of Westwoods, East Ogwell, to William Lambshead of Honeywell for £500. By 1861 the old farmhouse had been divided into two cottages in which lived (1) Peter Baker, 33, his wife Mary and their three children, Mary, Sarah and Jane and a boarder, Sarah Tarr, 14. (2) William Brewer, 25, his mother Ann, 50 and sister Susan, 20.

In 1864 Hindsground was purchased with other property by Alfred Lyon of Middlecott. The 1884 Ordnance Map shows the cottages, still habitable, fronting on to the River Lemon over which there was a footbridge and footpath leading up across the field to Smokey Cross.

The field called Three Corners along the Bickington Road and the woodland sold with it, was part of the unenclosed moorland of Honeywell Down, or Stapledon, up to the 18th, century. This piece of moorland stretched from the present positions of 'Widgers Down', Tor Garage to 'Owlsmead', and was the site of the manorial gallows of Ilsington Manor, hence the names of Stapledon (down marked with a post or stake), and Firchins (from furca, a forked stick), fields later enclosed out of it. Presumably the gallows were situated at the spot where the roads crossed on the moor, now called Smokey Cross, but named Firchins Cross in old books.

Many years after the enclosure of this moor there was still a wide piece of waste land on the left side of the road leading from Smokey Cross towards Haytor Down. When the parish wanted some land to build another dwelling in which to house the parish poor in 1828, they chose this bit of land and built a house there borrowing £100 from 'King Charlie' on the security of the parish rates. Eventually this house was converted into three cottages, and more recently into two cottages, Heather Cottage and Bracken Tor.

• HILL FARM •

A farm of Ingsdon Manor situated on the old London road, mentioned in 1330 in the Subsidy Roll as a farm. Little is known of its history until 1780 when it was owned by the Vinning family and later the Whidburns. Tenants since then have been Browning, White, Giles, Squires, Cornelius Caunter, John Balkwill, and Jonas Mitchell.

The farm was purchased by the Berry family of Barnstaple by 1840. Amalgamated into lands of Badcocks and Horton in the 1950s and ceased to be a separate farm.

• HOLBROOK •

Also named Olditch and Saddlecombe, Bretsland, Woodwalls. In the early 18th century this farm was taken out of the South Knighton farms and land inherited by Charles Wills of Town Barton from his wife Sarah Heller whose family farmed there. The house was rebuilt about 1830 by Charles Corbyn Wills. Farmed later by Mann and Symons families.

• HONEYWELL •

One of the tenements of Ilsington Manor where perhaps Stephen Honeywill farmed in 1332. In the 1566 survey William Wyger was the copyholder with the lord's land at Stapledon. His fields were Wonsbury 16 acres, Goodwell 12 acres, Easterpark 16 acres, Westerpark 8 acres and a field near the down called Stapledon 8 acres, and two closes called the Medes 2½ acres. It is interesting to note that the fields were very large at that time and a great deal of hedge building must have been done later. The Honeywill family are still living in the parish.

Honeywill was sold off form the Manor at its break up at the end of the 17th century. The Bowdon family had been tenants under the Manor for many years and apparently its first freehold owner-occupiers.

In 1726 Alexander Nosworthy conveyed it to a William Lambshead and it was owned by that family until 1864 when it was sold to Alfred Lyon of Middlecott. From the Lyon family it was sold to Samuel Thomas in the 1940s and then to Arthur Philp. Mr and Mrs Basil Philp are owner-occupiers today.

An interesting old farmhouse enlarged in the early 18th century, a little later than other local farmhouses, but it has not been altered much since, and still retains its thatch.

Honeywell farm-house c. 1930 is thought to have been enlarged in the 18th century. It is now farmed by the Philps.

• HORRIDGE •

There were two farms at Horridge, East and West, with the two farms adjoining – each having a very different history. East Horridge was owned by the Honeywill family and later the Kingwills, and West Horridge by the owners of Halshanger, the Nosworthys and Woodleys.

In the 1830s contention arose on Rippon Tor which finally resulted in a Court case in June 1834. Plaintiffs were Richard Kingwell who occupied West Horridge rented from James Woodley, and Nicholas Moale who occupied East Horridge, tenant of Richard Honeywill, and the defendant was John Rowell owner-occupier of one of the two farms at Mountsland.

The trouble arose because John Rowell claimed the right to drive sheep to stock his rights on Haytor Down from his enclosed Mountsland Common across Rippon Tor (the enclosed freehold of Horridge). It was a curious anomaly, the reason lost in the mists of antiquity, that the Mountslands were part of the Manor of Ilsington, and had rights on Haytor Down, although they were completely cut off from it by the Manor of Bagtor.

The title of the plaintiffs was of long standing, West Horridge being owned by the Woodleys for some 200 years and the Honeywills had owned East Horridge for upwards of 100 years. It was once part of the Manor of Bagtor and the Duke of Somerset was paid a small chief rent yearly.

In the early 20th century East was also bought by the Woodleys. Both were sold to William Whitley as part of his Buckland–Welstor estate, and tenanted by Easterbrooks and Smerdons. The farmhouse of East suffered an ignoble fate in the 1940s being used as an army practice by the Home Guard and American soldiers, and being totally demolished.

• ILSINGTON HEATHFIELD •

The large tract of heathland in the south-east of the parish called Ilsington Heathfield (some 500 acres) was enclosed by an Act of Parliament in 1809. It adjoined the heathlands of neighbouring parishes such as Bovey Tracey, Highweek and Teigngrace and was at one time a huge marshy area of several thousand acres, devoid of roads until it was drained in the 18th century.

Those who had common rights on the heathfield were allocated freehold pieces of it on its enclosure and other pieces were sold.

A large part of it, now the Great Plantation, became the property of the owners of Stover, but many of the cottages at Halford, Coldeast and Liverton, on the edge of the enclosure, lost their grazing and other common rights.

• INGSDON •

Ingsdon was one of the three main Domesday Manors of Ilsington. A Saxon, Frawin, held it before 1066, and it then passed to Osbern of Sacey, to the Paganels, Beaumonts and Pomeroys. Then to the Battishills, Tapsons and, about 1750, to Charles Hale who, it is said, met George Fursdon of Fursdon, Cadbury, while sheltering on Hampstead Heath during a thunderstorm and who he invited to visit Devon.

It remained in the Hale and Hale-Monro family (who replaced the Elizabethan Mansion with a Victorian one in 1867) until 1902 when it was sold to the White Sisters of St Brieuc in Brittany who ran a popular school there called St Michael's Convent. Due to a scarcity of Sisters to run the school it was sold and it became an approved school thereafter. It was destroyed by fire in 1977 and the old buildings were eventually demolished and several 'country houses' built on the estate.

INGSDON BURN

The barton or demesne lands of Ingsdon Manor were owned by the manor until 1902 when it was purchased by the Mann family, and more recently the Vooghts. The old farmhouse site has now been sold and the farm is now sited at the top of the hill and is run by Michael and Angela Vooght.

Views of Ingsdon Manor. Left: while it served as a convent school in the 1930s. Left below: *the smoke scarred entrance following the fire of 1977.* Below right: *The ruins of Ingsdon following the fire. Note the annex which was added to the Victorian house in the 1930s to provide for the education of convent children, many of them boarders.*

• LENDA •

Lenda was one of the early tenements of Ilsington Manor, with field names of Higher and Lower Barrow Fields which suggest pre-Saxon burials. It was still part of the manor in the 1566 survey and farmed by Robert Downing, however the mention of another building suggests that Lenda had been sub-divided. This was indeed the case by 1609 when 'Lynda' was leased to John Symons (aged 60) and Richard Bowdon.

At some stage the Manor sold the freehold, and in 1741 the Bowden's moiety was purchased by George Wills of Lustleigh, who had married Mary Corbyn, the heiress of Charles Corbyn of Higher Brimley, and the other moiety, then owned by the Mann family of Broadhempston, by Charles Corbyn himself. George Wills farmed both moieties, and in 1773 received the freehold of his father-in-law's part, on agreeing to provide for him in his old age. He also received other prop-

erties in the parish, Bickfords Tenement and Cose's in Ilsington Village, and fields at Liverton and Sigford. After the death of George Wills in 1788 the freehold of Lenda passed to Thomas Wills, his second son, who preferred to farm at Higher Brimley and it was let for several years. Eventually passing to George Wills, wine merchant of Bristol, it was sold in 1838 to his cousin Charles Corbyn Wills ('King Charlie') of Town Barton and returned to the main branch. It was the custom of the Wills family to marry their children to distant cousins, so keeping the land and the money in the family.

Lenda was sold again in the 1850s to a more distant family of Wills' cousins, and sometime in the late 1860s the old farmhouse and granary were destroyed by fire. I remember my great-aunt Mary, recalling as a young girl, seeing the corn in the granary exploding in the fire.

Rebuilt in the 1870s it continued to be owned by the Wills until about 1920 when it was sold to the Gill family of Ermington. Later becoming the home of the Hon. Mrs Coleridge and Phillpotts families, and farmed by Margaret and Ted Garrish, it is now owned by Paul and Liz Hewitt.

Lenda and Woodhouse Farms once formed part of the Manor of Ilsington and were claimed from the ancient forest with simple hand tools – what a feat! The site was chosen in a sheltered dip near to a spring. In the 18th century the author's grandfather, George Wills (1706–1788) of Hisley, Lustleigh parish, travelled five miles to marry his wife, Mary Corbyn of Lenda. Five miles in 300 years – not bad!

• LIVERTON VILLAGE •

Liverton (or Leveton) is ancient hamlet of Ilsington parish which began with the manor mill of Ilsington Manor. Water, scarce around Ilsington Village or Church Town, was collected from several streams by the time it got to Liverton, and here was built a mill to grind corn which grew on the Manor farms. When rainfall was low or there was a lot of milling to be done, water was collected in a mill-pond further up-stream, where it was let-out to turn the mill-wheel

In the early part of the 19th century there was a bridge at Liverton Mill over the stream, but the water from the leat driving the water-wheel ran over the road as a ford. The present Mill House was not then built and two cottages owned by James Woodley of Halshanger adjoined the detached garden opposite the Mill. Nearby Flower, or Floors, meadow suggests the site of a burning house for extracting the ore from the mines up the valley. Several farms and their cottages added to the hamlet congregated around the mill and the present Liverton Farm.

In the 19th century the hamlet increased its size when Henry Beare, an agricultural engineer, built a foundry here and a row of cottages for his workers, thinking that the main London–Penzance railway line would pass this way. At this time there were no buildings on the Newton Abbot road beyond Foundry Cottages, no shop or house opposite, and no Hayman's Cottages. However when Beare realised his mistake he moved his business to Newton Abbot, and a pottery took over his Liverton premises. This became the Devonmoor Art Pottery which employed some 40 persons until its closure in the 1950s.

Mrs Florrie Warren (née Doddridge) 1883–1976 in 1951 provided the author with the following recollections of Liverton:

I was born at the Star Inn in 1883. Water was very precious in those days for in a very hot summer the well would dry up and we had to fetch our water from a stream a half-mile away. Boiling the washing was done in an iron boiler over the tap-room fire. There was no sanitation.

The first means of transport I can remember was our donkey cart which we hired out. If the donkey refused to go we had a walk of five miles to Newton Abbot, and to carry home our shopping. Then my brother acquired a waggonette which he drove regularly to Newton on market days, and Mr John Potter succeeded him, buying a lorry which was used for carrying everything, and cleaned and provided with seats on Wednesdays. Life was beginning to take on a faster tempo and young people were visiting towns for their pleasure. Later Mr Potter bought a bus, which was then extended to one of the finest services of a privately owned fleet of buses in the West. Roads have seen a great improvement, the stony, dusty and irregular surfaces have been replaced by tarmac and many dangerous spots improved and widened.

The arrival of electricity has been a great boon, and telephones have been a great help. Also the availability of doctors and nurses for the sick and aged.

LIVERTON FARM

The original farm at Liverton formed the nucleus of the settlement, along with Liverton Mills. The farm became part of the Woodleys of Halshanger estate in the Liverton area and was let to Thomas Wotton, weaver in 1695. It was owned by Charles Wills of Town Barton at his death in 1790, and by his son Charles Corbyn Wills in 1840, and let to Jonas Mitchell. Farmed by William Badcock and Harry Horton in 1950s it ceased to be a farm in 1990s.

A view across Liverton from Penn Wood c. 1910, with Hillside cottage to the left.

Wood Cottages, Cummings Cross, Liverton. These dwellings were built at the cross roads after Ilsington Heathfield was enclosed by Act of Parliament in 1809. They were built by John Cumming after whom the cross roads were named. The Enclosure Act specified that the new roads over the Heathfield should be straight and at least 12 feet wide.

LIVERTON TITHE APPORTIONMENT IN 1839

No.	Holding Name	Description	Owner	Occupier
516	Goyle	Little Meadow	Duke of somerset	Wm.Skinner
517	Goyle	Orchard	Duke of Somerset	Wm. Skinner
518	Goyle	Garden	Duke of Somerset	Wm. Skinner
519	Goyle	Cottage & Linhay	Duke of Somerset	Wm. Skinner
520	Goyle	Orchard	Duke of Somerset	Wm.Skinner
522	Goyle	Garden	Duke of Somerset	Wm. Skinner
521	Woodgate Cottages	Orchard	Charles Corbyn Wills	John Thorn
523	Woodgate Cottages	Cottage & Garden	Charles Corbyn Wills	Wm. Emmett
524	Woodgate Cottages	Cottage & Garden	Charles Corbyn Wills	James Ridgeway
525	Woodgate Cottages	Cottage & Garden	Charles Corbyn Wills	Wm. Cock
526	Liverton Mill	Flowers Meadow	Charles Corbyn Wills	John Thorn
527		Garden	John Coleman	Henry Spry
528		Cottage & Garden	John Coleman	Henry Spry
529		Cottage & Garden	John Coleman	Joseph Setter
530		Cottage & Garden	Saml. Whiteway	James Bulley
531		Quillet	James Woodley	Mary Boarder
532		Cottage & Garden	James Woodley	Mary Boarder
533		Garden	James Woodley	Mary Boarder
534	Pitt Farm	Higher Pitt Meadow	James Woodley	Jonas Mitchell
535	Pitt Farm	Cottage & Garden	James Woodley	Jonas Mitchell
535a	Pitt Farm	Linhay & Yard	James Woodley	Jonas Mitchell
536	Pitt Farm	Lower Pitt Meadow	James Woodley	Jonas Mitchell
536a	Pitt Farm	Coppice	James Woodley	Jonas Mitchell
540		Kiln Close	James Woodley	Francis Rowell
541		Stable Field	James Woodley	Joseph Berry
542		Barley Arrish	James Woodley	Joseph Berry
659	Colesworthy	Great Old Hayes	James Woodley	John Rowell
660	Colesworthy	Little Old Hayes	James Woodley	John Rowell
661		Taylors Meadow	James Woodley	Jonas Mitchell
662	2 Tenements & Garden		James Woodley	John Hamlyn & Another
663	2 Tenements & Garden		James Woodley	Susan Coysh Francis Setter
664		Orchard	James Woodley	John Thorn
665		Cottage Barn &Yard	John Thorn	John Thorn
666		Garden	John Thorn	John Thorn
666a		Cottage & Garden	Thomas Widger	Wm. Prowse
667		Cottage & Garden	John Thorn	Wm. Coleman
668		2 Cottages, Yard & Stable	John Thorn	Wm. White & Another
669		Garden	John Thorn	Wm. White
670		Taylors Orchard	John Thorn	Jonas Mitchell
671		Cottage & Garden	C.C Wills	George Gilley
672		Cottage & Garden	C.C Wills	Wm. White
673		Inner Field	C.C Wills	Stephen Kingwill
674		Bothey	John Thorn	John Thorn
675		Old Orchard Field	C.C Wills	Stephen Kingwill
676		Road Field	C.C Willis	Stephen Kingwill
677		Beara Garden	John Thorn	John Thorn
716	Liverton Mills	Mill Garden	C.C Wills	John Thorn
717	Liverton Mills	Garden	James Woodley	Richard Smeardon
718		2 Cottages	James Woodley	Richard Smeardon
719		Liverton Mills	C.C Wills	John Thorn
720	Perrys Farm	Lower Perrys Meadow	James Woodley	John Thorn
720a	Perrys Farm	Barn & Linhay	James Woodley	John Thorn
714		Combe Hill		
724		Combe Meadow		
715		Hill Farm		

LIVERTON - DETAIL FROM THE TITHE MAP OF 1839

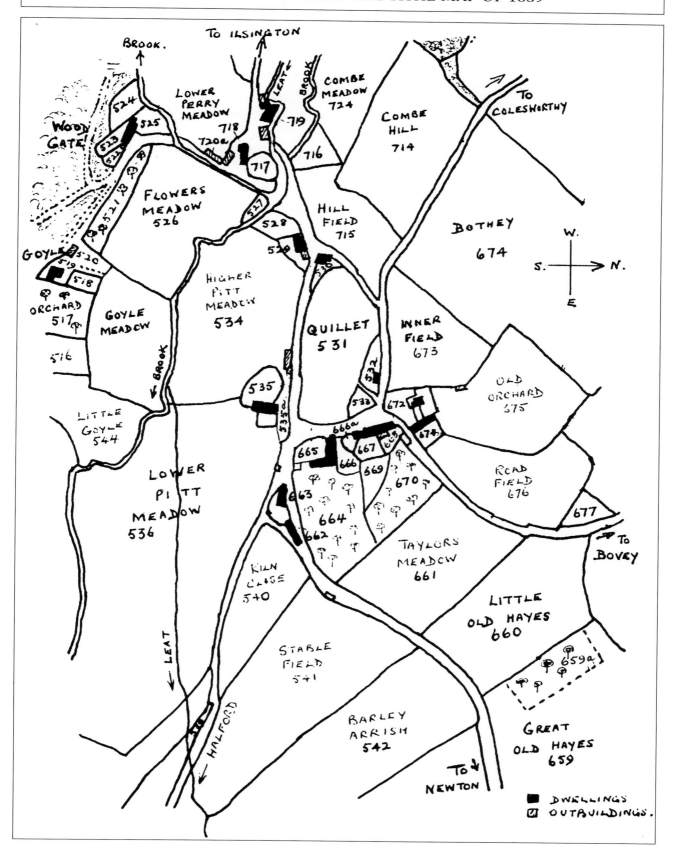

LIVERTON

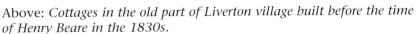

Above: *Cottages in the old part of Liverton village built before the time of Henry Beare in the 1830s.*

Left: *Another of the older cottages at Liverton, probably dating from the 17th century. The village well and pump stands by the door. Note the thatched roof and elm-boarded gable end.*

Below: *Liverton c.1920. The cottages, workshops and residential house were built in the 1840s by the engineer Henry Beare after he came to Liverton from Meeth in North Devon. Here he manufactured agricultural machinery and tools until he moved his works to Newton Abbot in order to be close to the railway.*

• LOUNSTON •

Lounston lies in a valley to the south of Ilsington Village which 30 years ago contained four farms, Great, Lower, Higher East and Lower East Lounston, and no other houses. In those days and very likely for centuries it was almost self-contained agriculturally. Now it has vastly changed. Farms have sold off land to neighbours, barns have been converted into dwellings and a complete new community has emerged.

LOWER LOUNSTON (SX786750)

Also known as Oxenhams, Longs, Zellacks or Welshes. In the early 18th century it was owned by the Oxenham family who had inherited it from the Longs. A deed of 1750, when the farmhouse was called 'a decayed house formerly a barn', mentions it had been the property of the Sellacks, a family frequently mentioned in the church registers in the 16th and 17th centuries, their name appearing on an old tombstone in the broom cupboard of the Tower Vestry (the author

once suggested to someone that this unusual location would preserve the stone longer than it being in the chancel and received the reply that the deceased may have been a witch!).

The farm was let to a series of tenants, including Matthias Rowell in the late 18th century and George Paddon. The Oxenhams sold to the Aclands, who sold it to John Welch (who had to pay extra chief-rent to the Lord of the Manor in 1824 for enclosing some waste land). It was sold again in 1837 to Wm Langley and then to the Martins, Lillingtons and Martyn-Lillingtons who sold to Walter Dymond in 1921. The Dymonds sold to Gerald Pilkington in 1977.

In more recent times the farmhouse and buildings have been converted into dwellings and sold, but the land remains intact owned by Gerry and Valerie Pilkington and is farmed as accommodation land by their son Mark.

There was an adjoining farm to this at SX786749, called Little Lounston, Leats or Honeywills, whose history can be traced further

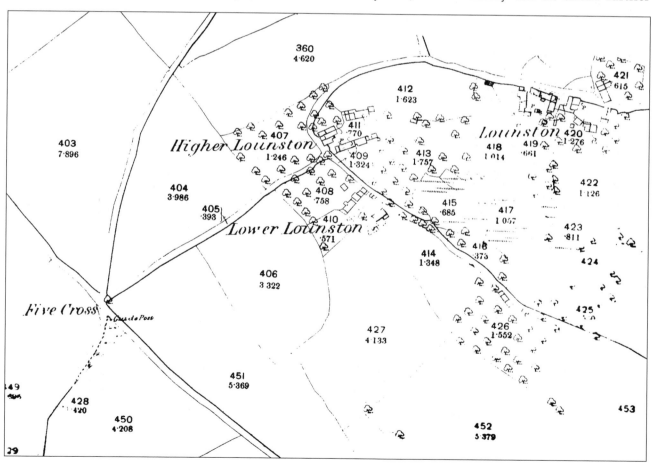

Lounston from the Ordnance Survey map of 1884.

back. A document of 1594 says the property was once the inheritance of Lord Compton and later of Thomas Southcott. In the 1566 survey Helena Mann had held it by copyhold since 1526, and Agneta Hart held it before that. The copyhold passed to her son Robert Mann who had purchased the freehold before his death in 1609, then to his son Walter, who died in 1615, and his widow Alice who sold to John Bowdon of Honeywell in 1617. In 1624 Bowdon sold to William Leate of Ilsington, husbandman, in whose family it remained for many years, passing to the Taylors and Kingwills in 1780. By 1785 Jonas Honeywill became the owner-occupier and he sold to William Langley, merchant of Teignmouth, in 1850. He was also the owner of the adjoining farm and from this time the old farmhouse became derelict. All traces of it had disappeared by the 1884 Ordnance Survey.

GREAT LOUNSTON (SX784751)

Also called South Lounston and part of the Manor of Ilsington which was tenanted by the Furlongs, the ownership seems to have passed to the Drakes from the Fords. In 1783 it was advertised for sale with a good farmhouse, 3 acres of orchard, 230 acres of arable, pasture, etc. in possession of Thomas Bickford tenant. It was sold to William Nosworthy of Ford, Manaton, and tenanted by the Kingwills and Mortimores. On Nosworthy's death in 1820 it passed to his son Rev. Stephen Nosworthy who was curate of Widecombe and Rector of Buckland Filleigh. Whilst in his ownership, on Saturday April 12th 1834, the farmhouse at Great Lounston, occupied by George Mortimer, was burned to the ground.

The fire, discovered at 6am, burned out by 8.30am.

From 1873 John and George Wills late of Ideford became tenants, later the Berrys. In 1920 Nosworthys sold to the Berrys and the Berrys to Clifford Sanders in 1955. It is now farmed by Michael and Shirley Sanders and Gordon Sanders.

HIGHER EAST LOUNSTON (SX786751)

Also called Wills' Lounston and Hills' Lounston. In 1780 owned by George Wills of Rudge, Lustleigh, and let to Michael Rowell.

It continued in the ownership of the Wills of Rudge and Kelly until another George Wills died in 1875 and left it to his widow who married Admiral Hill of Newton Abbot, and it remained in the Emma Hill trust until sold to F. Knapman in the 1960s, then to David and Christine Bardell in the 1990s.

LOWER EAST LOUNSTON (SX787751)

Also called Winsors', Lays', Shapters or East Lounston. In 1780 it was owned by Mrs Winsor let to John Eady. Later tenants were Isaac Ford, the Bastows, and the Rowells for nearly a century. Then by Nicholas Moalle and Willcocks who also owned it. It was sold to Rudolf Neufeldt about 1946. He sold land north of the road to neighbour Fred Knapman about 1965.

The farmhouse was likely to have been rebuilt by the Shapters on the south side of the road who had their residence there as well, and the old farm seems to have been on the north side of the road with the building protruding into the road (see O.S. 1884 maps).

• MIDDLECOTT •

One of the farms of the Manor of Ilsington on its northern boundary. It was started with the clearing of the woodland, and scrub, very likely in Saxon times. By the time of the 1566 Survey of Ilsington Manor it was let by copyhold to Elizabeth Bruseigh and in 1609 by Hugh Ferys and Humphrey Lambshead. Sold by the Manor in the 1680s it became property of the Leare family of Narracombe and descended to the Codnor and Searle side of the family. Sold by them to John Cumming who owned it in 1780 and to the Rowells, farmers of Ilsington and builders of Teignmouth, who added the Georgian front to the farmhouse. It was sold by them to Alfred Lyon of Timperley in 1864 who added to the house and laid out the gardens as a gentleman's residence. He lived there until 1898 and it then passed to Thomas Henry Lyon, his son, who was a well known architect. Inhabited by him until his death in 1953 it passed to Baker-Smith, and sold in 1955 to Alex Ware. It is now the residence of George and Yvonne Ware-Owen.

Middlecott was formerly a farm which was purchased by Alfred Lyon a former tea merchant in India and a Manchester factory owner. The house became his residence and he purchased other farms in the area with an eye to the development of the mining industry, but these plans came to nothing.

• MOUNTSLAND •

Two ancient farms existed at Mountsland at SX759740 for generations, anciently part of the Manor of Bagtor, and apparently both were sold from the Manor in the early 17th century or before.

ENDACOTTS OR ROWELLS' MOUNTSLAND

The earliest date recorded is from the Ilsington Church registers when John Prowse de Mounsland was buried in 1589. Then the Taylor family farmed it for several years, and another record dated 1676 exists when Arthur Langworthy purchased it from John Hawkins of Dartington, and adds that it had lately been in the possession of Julian Widdecombe and Elizabeth Palke.

The mention of Langworthy is interesting, and it appears that he gave the name to the present Langworthy Brook. In 1677 Langworthy let the farm to Thomas Whittley of Ilsington, bachelor, on the life of Whittley and John Endacott, son of Thomas of Ilsington. So began the long associa-

tion with the Endacott family, until it passed to the Rowells through marriage about 1795 and stayed in that family to about 1890 when it was sold to the Woodleys of Halshanger. The Easterbrooks then became tenants and the property was sold in 1923 to the Whitleys and became part of the Buckland–Welstor estate.

KINGWILL'S MOUNTSLAND

In 1668 Robert Hawkins of Berry Pomeroy left his share of Mountsland to John Hawkins of Dartington, and in 1676 he sold it to Arthur Langworthy. There are no records of how or when he disposed of it, but the next record is 1780 when John Kingwill was owner-occupier. In 1796 it was divided between his two sons William and Richard, the latter building a new house and selling his share to Woodley of Halshanger in 1835. The other share descended to William Pearse who sold to Woodleys in 1901. Tenants the Easterbrooks. Sold to the Whitleys in 1923.

• OLDERTOWN •

A small farm between Smallacombe and Middlecott bordering on the moor. Owned by the Kingwill family for several years, until being incorporated into Smallacombe. Farmhouse became cottage. In 1566 held by Agnes Orchard, widow, from the manor by copyhold. Several fields called Shotts, the old strip lands in medieval times. In the 1880s the old thatched farmhouse burnt down, and eventually was rebuilt on the west side of the lane from the moor.

• PINCHAFORD •

A mainly unaltered Dartmoor farm longhouse until the disastrous fire of 1944 when the thatched building was entirely gutted. The fire took place in an exceptionally cold period when roads were slippery and snowbound, and water froze in the hoses. In spite of this the fire brigades were at first directed to a situation some miles away, and when they eventually got to Pinchaford, there was little that could be done.

This was an ancient Saxon holding, part of the Manor of Ilsington, which was, with Woodhouse, the last two farms to be sold away from the Manor in the early 19th century.

The tenants of the farm, paid a very low rent to the manor, because of their duty in charge of the manor pound, where stray animals were impounded, until their freedom was redeemed by their owners.

Pinchaford Farm c. 1900. The dwelling is a typical Devon longhouse of the 16th century.

• POOL •

This smallholding takes its name from the mill pool which lay in the valley above Liverton Mill. Here water was collected and released to drive the mill wheel.

Pool was owned by the Widger family and later by the Wills family.

• RORA •

Rora is situated in the eastern part of Ilsington, a holding of ancient vintage and part of the demesne or barton lands of Ilsington Manor. The name Rora is very likely derived from the Celtic word 'or' meaning a boundary, and we know that the lands of the Saxon lord Peadington passed near this spot, as well as it being on the manorial boundary. The farm was tenanted by the Northway family for many years, and its ownership descended with the rest of Ilsington Manor. It escaped the break up of the manor in the late 17th century and remained with the Ford/Filmore family until sold by the Phillpotts to Mr and Mrs McIntyre in the 1960s.

• SANCTUARY •

The name Sanctuary or Sentry comes from the early English name for 'Glebe' meaning land and property belonging to the church, as opposed to property owned by the Manor.

With the gift of church property at Ilsington by Henry VIII to his chapel of St George at Windsor, the tithes of Ilsington were divided into rectorial tithes owned by Windsor, and the vicarial tithes owned by the local church. So for many years the Sanctuary was known as 'The Rectory' adjoining 'The Vicarage' next door.

For many years the Sanctuary was farmed with its own lands and the glebelands belonging to the Vicarage which were generally known as 'The Sheaf'. When tithes were commutated it was eventually sold to Charles Corbyn Wills, who already owned most of the cottages in Ilsington Village.

The Sanctuary then passed to Mrs Rowell of Bradninch whose daughter sold it to the tenant Mrs Carpenter, in 1938. The present owners are Robert and Dinah Milne.

The Sanctuary, Ilsington, at one time known as the Rectory House.

• SIGFORD •

Sigford was a small Domesday Manor held by Soloman under Roald Dubbed, a Norman supporter of the Conqueror who held several manors in Devon including Wonford. Before the Conquest it was held by a Saxon called Brictric. In the Middle Ages Sigford was included in the Hundred of Wonford, as was its neighbouring manor of Bagtor. The hamlet of Lower Sigford is situated near the confluence of the three streams of Langworthy Brook, the Sig and the Lemon, and had its own manor mill.

Several farms have existed in the hamlet of Sigford through the past millennium and it is difficult to pick out their whereabouts and the names can be very confusing. Not until the tithe survey of 1839 accompanied by the tithe map, can we definitely pick out their position and the fields which belonged to each farm.

LOWER SIGFORD

The present farm of Lower Sigford (SX 779739) is owned and farmed by David and Pat Coysh. This can be positively identified as the farm called Hales or Hearles, Middle Sigford and Wills' Sigford at different times of its history. Owned by the Smallacombe branch of the Wills for many years, it was bought by the Berrys in 1842 and then by the Firths of Ashburton. Tenants were W. S. Nicholls.

HIGHER SIGFORD

At SX781744, it is said, in 1741, to have been owned by Richard Leare. There is a granite stone over the fireplace in one of the bedrooms carved with the date 1665. It was owned by the Woodleys of Halshanger in 1780 to the 20th century and let to the Mortimores. It was then sold to John Clark and inherited by Mortimores and the farm split between two daughters, Pearl Crossman and Maisie Cock.

SWEET'S SIGFORD

At SX781745 this settlement was also called Clog's, Cloy's and Hales. In 1780 it was owned by Jane Newberry, who married a William John Hale of Chudleigh, and let to Edward Leaman. It was sold to John Sweet in 1798 and to the Woodleys by 1810. The lands were joined to Higher Sigford and the farmhouse became a cottage and was later

View of the Lemon valley towards Lower Sigford, with Bagtor Wood on the right horizon.

Sigford House, formerly known as Widdicombe's Sigford.

abandoned, although it is still standing in the cattle yard.

NORTH SIGFORD

At SX776752, the farmhouse stood near the present Higher Sigford Cottages. Also called Charles Wills' Sigford, it is now part of Honeywell Farm.

Owned by Charles Wills of Town Barton for many years the farmhouse was demolished before 1839. Sold to William Lambshead in 1860 and again to Alfred Lyon of Middlecott in 1864. The land lay west of the Haytor-Bickington road in the manor of Sigford/Bagtor.

SIGFORD MILL

At SX777738, this was the ancient manorial mill of the manor of Sigford. Now amalgamated into Sigford House property. It could well be synonymous with Pitts Lower Sigford.

HANNAFORD'S SIGFORD

From the tithe survey it is pinpointed as being part of the garden opposite the present Sigford cottages at SX777737. Perhaps it was the Manor House of Sigford, anciently the home of a branch of the Fords. The house was demolished at some time in the Victorian era and the land taken over by neighbouring farms. Tenanted by Leaman family at end of 18th century.

PITTS LOWER SIGFORD

This dwelling seems to have been close to Hannaford's Sigford at SX777737, and again may have been Sigford Manor House. Owned by Nosworthy family in the 17th century and sold to the Widgers about 1782 by Samuel Nosworthy of Narracombe.

OXENHAM'S SIGFORD

Oxenham's Sigford, at SX776737, is also called West Sigford, Long's and Cater's was owned by the Oxenham family until 1820 when it was bought by the Widgers and descended to the Boveys. Farmed by the Caters, Widgers, Manns, and Fowlers, it was later sold to the Willcocks who sold in 1965 to George Owen and Dick Wills (the author), and the farmhouse to W. Bosence, and sold again to Bill Williams and Maurice Retallick. The farmhouse is now called Oxenhams, and the land reverting to the name of an ancient holding in the Grove, Harkworthy.

WIDDICOMBE'S SIGFORD
OR SIGFORD HOUSE

WIDDICOMBE'S SIGFORD OR SIGFORD HOUSE

Sigford House, at SX777740, is now the home of Mrs Joan Evans. It was owned in the 17th century by the Widdicombe family and let at times to Hanniball Corbyn, Gunston and Furlong. By 1775 it had become the property of the Widgers and continued in that family until sold by their descendants, the Boveys, in the early 20th century, and later passed to Peter Whitley and Colin Evans.

• STONE CRACKER'S ROOST •

Also known as Moorland View, Little Stapledon, and Ollerton, this was the house built at Smokey Cross in the early 1920s by George Roberts. It was called 'Stonecracker's Roost' by the locals in a taunting manner for they believed that George, who earned his living by cracking stones for use on the roads, was getting above his station by building a house for himself.

It is interesting to note that the site on which the house stands must have been close to the site of the manor gallows, and near to where those executed were buried.

Stone Cracker's Roost.

• SOUTH KNIGHTON •

SOUTH KNIGHTON HOUSE (HINGSTONS)

At one time, at the end of the 19th century, this dwelling was called the Elms, but the 1839 tithe survey refers to it as Hingston. It was owned by the Bickford family for many years, then by George Wills of Narracombe before being sold back to Henry Bickford.

SOUTH KNIGHTON FARM

In 1780 there were two main farms at South Knighton, one Hingstons (now South Knighton House), and Ushers opposite, both owned by the Bickford family. There were several smallholdings, one owned by Richard Widger, Fursmans owned by John Motton, Springwells by Christopher Cater, and Cains by John Northcott.

There are existing deeds from the early 17th century but the properties and fields are very confused from the period until 1780.

As with all the hamlets in Ilsington parish they started off with several farms surrounded with the cottages where their employees lived, but now, except perhaps for Sigford, all have lost their farms and their farmhouses. The cottages have become residential and the farm buildings converted into homes.

Lenda

• SMALLACOMBE •

Smallacombe is one of the old farms of Ilsington Manor situated on its borders with the moor and no doubt settled in Saxon times, and possibly before. At the time of the Domesday survey Ralf Paganel the owner of Ilsington had 22 villeins and probably one of these farmed Smallacombe.

The first recorded reference is in 1342 when it was written as Smalecombe. In the 1566 survey of the manor Hugh Dyggen or Degon farmed Smallacombe paying to the lord an annual rent of 48s 8d, and a load of hay. It is interesting that the names of the fields include Lewthorne Park and Tromptsmede from which Trumpeter is derived. The Smerdon family took over from the Degons as copyholders. When the manor broke up either the Smerdons or Wills purchased it. John Wills who came to Ilsington from Lustleigh in one of their several overspills, was the owner at the beginning of the 18th century, and for the next 150 years that family owned and farmed there. Joseph Wills who was there at the beginning of the 19th century was the grandfather of William John Wills the Australian explorer.

William Lambshead purchased the farm in 1860 and sold to entrepreneur Alfred Lyon in 1863 when the old thatched farmhouse was a burned out shell. He rebuilt the house and he and his son let the farm for the next 80 years when it was sold to the Bradfords, later to the Thomases, and to Peter and Connie Klinkenberg in 1948.

• STANCOMBE •

In 1630 John Degon and John Hillinge paid Church Rates for Stancombe. In 1780 there were three farms at Stancombe, Great and Higher Stancombe owned by John Wolston and let to William Laskey, and Lower Stancombe owned by Thomas Seal and farmed by Charles Wills. By 1839 all three Stancombes were owned by the Rev. Christopher Wolston (112 acres) and farmed by William Northcott, Thomas Ford, and sold to Jonas Mitchell and let to Samuel Wrayford.

• LOWER STAPLEHILL •

The ancient family of Archer farmed Lower Staplehill all through the 17th century and perhaps later. There is a ledger stone on the floor of the porch before the main door of St Michael's Parish Church, Ilsington, in memory of John Archer of Staplehill who died in 1672, it contains the following inscriptions: 'Earth take my body, keep it safe, my soul thou cans't not have. It's gone to Heaven and rests above, in spite of Hell or Grave.' In 1780 Lord Clifford of Chudleigh was the owner and Peter Mann the tenant. In 1810 the property was bought by James Templer and in 1829 sold with the rest of the Stover Estate to the Duke of Somerset. It was later occupied by Joseph Edwards and after by the Rowells and Newcombes. Higher Staplehill lies in Highweek Parish

Town Barton

• TOWN BARTON •

Town Barton one of the two farms in Ilsington Village was also known as Town Farm and Sheare's Tenement, and at one time during the ownership of William Rowell, who farmed the lands of Town Barton and Court Barton, he incorrectly called the whole farm Court Barton. The Sheare family lived in the parish during the 17th and 18th centuries. But when Town Barton was sold from the Manor is not known.

The house burnt down about 1870. The Symons or Simmons family (the origin of Simms Hill) seem to have been freeholders as early as the early 17th century.

In 1844 the Wills family sold Town Barton which they and their forebears the Corbyn family had farmed and owned for about a hundred years. The purchaser was Charles Hale-Monro of Ingsdon who already owned the other Ilsington village farm, Court Barton, which had been joined to Town Barton for about thirty-five years and farmed by Charles Corbyn Wills senior, 'King Charlie'.

The author recently found the following advertisements in *Trewman's Exeter Flying Post*, the local newspaper of the time:

Mr. G. Hooper junior has been instructed to sell by Public Auction on Monday, Tuesday and Thursday, the property of Mr. Charles Corbyn Wills who has sold the farm and is about to quit.

513 sheep, 56 bullocks, 17 horses and colts, 19 pigs, 6 ricks of old and new hay (the produce of 58 acres), 6 acres of potatoes in lots, 14 packs of excellent wool, good selection of husbandry implements (some on improved principles), 10 hogsheads of good cider, and casks and empty casks of oak and elm timber, ditto board, 1000 faggots of oak coppice wood, several ricks of hedge and cleft wood, 200 young apple trees fit for planting without, young ditto and gribbles, dairy utensils and household furniture.

Particulars described in Handbills.

1st day's sale. Livestock, hay, straw, apple trees, wool and poultry.

2nd day. Husbandry implements, cider and casks, empty casks, oak and elm timber, ditto board, wood and potatoes.

3rd day. Household furniture and dairy utensils.

The Auctioneer in calling the attention of his agricultural friends and the public generally to the extensive and valuable sale of farming stock, begs to say it will be found worthy of attention, and the same being so well known, any comment on it would be superfluous. Refreshment on the table the first day at 11 o'clock and the sale to commence punctually at half past 12. On the 2nd and 3rd days the sale will commence punctually at 2. Dated at Withecombe, Chagford. August 7th, 1844.

• TRUMPETER •

Derived from the name Tromptsmede (the meadow of one called Trump), mentioned in a deed enrolled on 2 Feb. 1568. It was mortgaged by George Forde of Ilsington esquire, to Leonard Miller of Ilsington, yeoman, 'for 5000 of good white tin for the moiety of lands called Smallacombe and half of a meadow of land called Tromptsmede, all of which are in the tenure of Hugh Degon. To be void if George repays the tin at the Queen's Beam at Ashburton on April 1st next.'

In the 1566 survey of Ilsington Manor the lands of Smallacombe contain a field called Tromptsmede, one acre in size. Hugh Degon paying 48 shillings and 8 pence and a load of hay yearly rental.

The two cottages at SX778764 were farm cottages owned by Smallacombe Farm, but the other two cottages to the north, originated as the Atlas Mining company's office on the first floor and underneath a shed and stable. The four cottages were reconstructed by Capt. C. H. Quelch in 1939.

• WESTERBROOK •

Westerbrook was a smallholding of Bagtor Manor for several centuries which often was farmed with the moorland farm of Emsworthy. Tenants include the Winsor family and later, after 1896, George Tickell who augmented farming with producing paving stones, kerbs and sets from granite moorstone and, unfortunately, the easier obtained stones from cairns and hut-circles. The old thatched house was completely destroyed by fire in 1924 and rebuilt with the land amalgamated with Bagtor Barton. The house is now owned by Doug and Karen Smith.

• WILLSWORTHY •

Also known as Willsery or anciently as Willescrew this farm was in the manor of Ilsington and not Langaller as may have been thought. It is mentioned in the 1630 church rate assessment as being farmed by Tristram Watts, and in 1694 as having been leased by Alexander Hill to Charles Trengrove a mercer of Bovey Tracey, and having been sold to him in 1705.

In 1725 Trengrove sold to Thomas Comyns of Wood, Bishopsteignton. By 1780 it was owned by John Rogers and let to a series of tenants, Richard Perryman, Mary Maye of Brimley, William Scott and Daniel Harvey. Eventually it was sold to John Divett, the Bovey Pottery owner and to the Church Commissioners, who no doubt rebuilt the new house there, after a fire destroyed the old thatched one. The land was amalgamated with Langaller.

• WOODHOUSE •

Woodhouse was one of the last farms of the Manor of Ilsington to be sold and it was not until 1838, one hundred and fifty years after the break-up of most of the manor lands, that William Mortimore purchased it from Emlin Filmore, the lady of the manor. It had been let to the Lambsheads, Joseph Wills of Smallacombe, and Richard Perryman. The Mortimores sold to Bill Rowell about 1920 and it has been sold to William Harvey, Dr Walter Scott, Mrs Dixon and is now owned by Brett and Kieran Day. Most of the land has been sold to John Hendy of Colesworthy.

Right: *The author as a boy and farmworker Bill Derges watch a cow eating cake from a bucket c.1929. Mr Derges (as the author always knew him) had worked at Narracombe since 1903 and lived at Higher Brimley. He always had a joke and lady visitors were always pleased to see him. He was a good judge of character and would whisper a joke in their ear, resulting in streams of laughter. He was born, of all places, in Paddington Green, London, his parents having emigrated from North Bovey. Bill ran away to sea at an early age but one voyage across the Channel to Dunkirk was enough for him and when the vessel put in again at Teignmouth he jumped ship, ending up with his grandparents at North Bovey. Ever after he would talk about 'when I was at sea'. He had a large family, four girls and three boys, and worked part-time well past retirement age.*

15 - Narracombe - Portrait of a Farm

Narracombe or Northacombe, its earliest name, had very likely as its name suggests, a Saxon beginning, formed very soon after the Manor of Ilsington. It stands on the manor's northern edge to protect its boundaries and to clear the thick virgin woods and scrubland which covered the whole area. The clearance and the formation of the farm and its enclosures would have taken generations, working just with hand tools. We do not know the names of the inhabitants of those early years, presumably they were villeins of the manor, holding the farm by copyhold from the lords of the manor whose names are known.

The first family we do know that held Northacombe, were those who held it long enough in the 14th century, to be given the surname of 'de Northacombe'. (Earlier than this the ordinary villagers did not have surnames, but were largely known by nicknames, such as John the smith, or Tom the son of Will etc.).

The years went by and the first Leare that we know of, came on the scene. By this time, the Leares had become a prolific and quite well off. They owned land around Ilsington, Bovey and Ashburton, and had family branches at Totnes, Staverton and Ipplepen. One of the Ipplepen family emigrated to Barbados in the late 16th century and made his fortune in sugar. Returning at the Restoration of the monarchy, he was honoured with a baronetcy.

The Ilsington branch of the family were perhaps less venturesome and preferred to be farmers, one of these, Richard, is mentioned in the Arundell documents (holders of $^1/_4$ part of Ilsington Manor) as renewing his lease on Northacombe sub Coudre (translated by Valerie Ransom as 'Northacombe under the hazel coppice') in 1591. From then until 1672 the Leares remained copyholders of Northacombe from the manor, but by that time the manor lands were beginning to be sold and they purchased the freehold, with extensive rights of common on Haytor Down. Haytor Down had always been part of Ilsington Manor; parts of it were enclosed from time to time during the centuries and some of the manorial lords used their rights to work it for minerals, the remaining parts were used as summer grazing for the lord's and his tenant's animals. When the farms were sold, the new freeholders were allocated common rights on the moorland, with an annual payment of a peppercorn rent, called a chief-rent, to the manor for ever (this was abolished in 1935).

As was the custom the Leares arranged marriages for their children among the local farming community, and married them to their distant cousins to prevent the land and the money from going out of the family. Thus the Wills of Lustleigh, the Nosworthys of Manaton, the Corbyns of Ilsington, etc., all became one extended family, and there were not many farms in the area which did not have some connection. When the Narracombe Leares did not have a son in 1754, their daughter Elizabeth married cousin Samuel Nosworthy of Caseley in Lustleigh. When Samuel Nosworthy of Narracombe and his wife, who had been Mary Wills of Smallacombe, were left with three daughters in 1808, their eldest married George Wills of Higher Brimley, Ilsington, and so brought the two adjoining farms of Narracombe and Higher Brimley together.

RICHARD LEARE

The following schedule is attached to the deed of the marriage settlement of Richard Leare of Narracombe and Joan Wills of Lustleigh in 1702. The inventory is interesting for the value put on things we would consider trivial items today: dishes and pans, and barrels and keeves. It shows how they valued cider.

A schedule of all such household goods, stock, cattle and corn as is or are intended to be conveyed by the deeds to which this schedule is annexed:

200 sheep and lambs, 16 bullocks, 10 acres of wheat, barley, oats and peas, 6 swine hogs, 2 horses, 10 pewter dishes, 6 brass pans, 4 beds and bedstands, 5 hogsheads, 3 barrels, 2 brass crocks, 1 chest, 1 press, 3 keeves, 2 table-boards, 1 treadle, 1 standard, 1 flagon.

Left: *Narracombe front garden today.*

Below: *Narracombe farm buildings in the snow c.1934. The range in the background was built for my grandfather Charles W. Wills (1854–1921) in 1898 by Hugh Mills of Newton Abbot. Granite for the building came from the Haytor quarries and the total cost was £400. The small building to the right was the wood linhay (underneath) where faggots of wood for the hearth fire, and logs for the other fires, were kept. It also usually housed a ferret hutch.*

NARRACOMBE FARM

A short history of Narracombe Farm since 1880 is as follows :

The author's grandfather Charles William Wills, married Amy Braim, the youngest daughter of the vicar of Ilsington in April 1880. He was the only surviving son of George and Susanna Wills and had two sisters. Charles and Amy had a family of two sons and three daughters, and on his death in 1921 his property was divided between them.

My father Sydney, inherited Narracombe with conditions, and his brother Charlie inherited his paternal grandmother's family farm of Daccombe in Coffinswell. My father and mother, Sydney and Mary Rendell of Kingston, Staverton, married in 1911, and had three boys, Charlie, Frank and myself (Dick). Again, on my father's death in 1947, a year after I was demobbed from the RAF, Narracombe was bequeathed to the three of us. My younger brother was an architect, and the other two of us were required to buy his share, and in consequence we formed a partnership to run the farm. In 1954, seven years later, my elder brother died unexpectedly, and I continued in partnership with his widow, Mollie, until my nephew Robert then aged 4, became 21.

In 1971 Robert and I continued the partnership, selling land at Sigford which we had purchased to increase the farm's size in 1965, to buy cows and build a milking parlour, and to change the herd from South Devons to Friesians. In 1983 because of new regulations for dairy farms, we decided to sell the herd and milk quota we held. Robert started a business of his own in bull genetics and for a year or so we let the grass.

In 1986 I started a new enterprise with Ed Williams, renting Narracombe and part of Sigford, and keeping South Devon suckler cows. From a beginning of one cow, we built up a herd of 120 cows in ten years, with 200 followers, buying an extra 16 acres of land adjoining Narracombe, at Middlecott, over another five years.

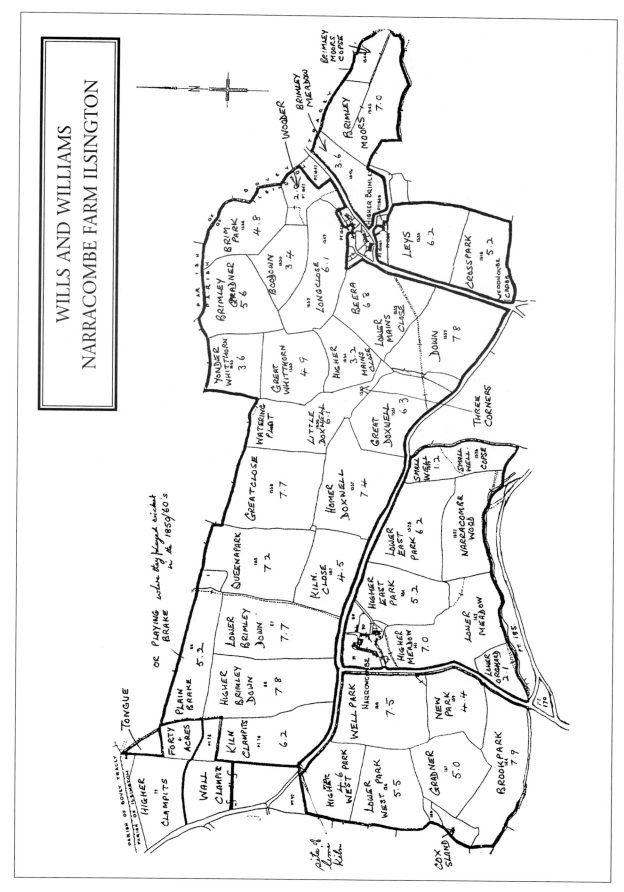

WILLS AND WILLIAMS
NARRACOMBE FARM ILSINGTON

Plan of Narracombe farm in 1995 showing field names and acreages. Many of the fields have the same names they carried in the 16th and 17th centuries.

Narracombe fields from the bottom of Middlecott Hill to the fields below Higher Brimley. The fields are as follows: 1. Furzehills, 2. Higher West Park, 3. Lower West Park, 4. Newpark Gratna, 5. Well Park, 6. Kiln Clampitts, 7. Higher Brimley, 8. Plain Brake, 9. Lower Brimley Down, 10. Queenapark, 11. Great Close, 12. Watering Plot, 13. Meadow, 14. Higher East Park, 15. Kiln Close, 16. Homer Doxwell, 17. Lower East Park, 18. Smallwell, 19. Yonder Whitthorn, 20. Great Whitthorn, 21. Higher Mainclose, 22. Brimpark Boodown, 23. Longclose, 24. Great Doxwell, 25. Lower Mainclose, 26. Down, 27. Brook Park, 28. Lower Meadow, 29 Narracombe Wood. A - Green Lane. B - Narracombe. C - Ilsington Village. D - Bovey Tracey. All aerial photographs were taken by Ed Williams, July 1997.

During the Second World War searchlight batteries were dotted around the countryside to confuse German fliers as to the whereabouts of important targets. One such battery was at Sigford, another at Ullacombe Farm on the Bovey–Haytor road. On the night of the Exeter blitz in 1941 parachute flares were dropped by German aircraft over the Green Lane area to investigate isolated buildings. The author picked up several large silk parachutes next day, in the locations marked 'x' on the photograph. The numbers refer to the field names given above.

The landscape, farms, and dwellings around Middlecott. 1. Bel Alp, 2. Oldertown, 3. Smallacombe, 4. Ladymead, 5. Middlecott, 6. Green Lane, 7. Trumpeter, 8. Moonraker, 9. Lewthorn, 10. Ilsington Hotel, 11. Ilsington playing field, 12. Portland Villa.

Narracombe from the air, 1997.

View from Doxwell Stile towards Narracombe Farmhouse and Haytor Rocks. To the left on the horizon is Rippon Tor and Pinchaford Ball. The lane in the centre (a continuation of Green Lane) was the manor boundary of Ilsington (to the left) and Brimley (to the right), perhaps the lands of the Earl of Richmond and, at Domesday, the Thane of Pullabrook. The two fields of Doxwell are on the right - the smallholding being part of Brimley Manor which was purchased by the author's great (four times) grandfather, Samuel Nosworthy, who added it to Narracombe. It is thought that its cottage stood near the site of the oak tree, centre left.

The view from Lower Brimley Down Field at Narracombe. On the left is Newton Abbot with Trago Mills and Blackpool School in the nearer valleys. The Ingsdon hills stand in the centre with the conical hill of Penn Wood or Mount Pisca, near centre.

Narracombe Farmhouse in the foreground and the view looking south to the line of hills behind Totnes, and Ramshorn Down in the centre.

The Georgian Front was added in 1837, but a view of the north-east end clearly shows the original line of the house, which was formerly a long-house construction. The bottom end or shippen was single storey and was only raised c.1750 when the slate replaced the thatched roof. In 1837 a major rebuilding phase began, and the eaves were straightened up.

The black lines shows the profile of the thatch before the building of the 1837 extension and reveals the outline of the longhouse. Narracombe was originally serviced with two drinking water supplies, a pump by the Ash-House and a spring at the Court-gate. The lavatory was supplied by rainwater which fell on the roof. Following an outbreak of scarlet fever in 1883, the spring water was piped to near the wood linhay and then the dairy. In 1922 mains water was taken in via the back door.

Narracombe from the east side before the garage was built in 1921. The tree on the right was a Portugal laurel brought home in his pocket by the author's great-grandfather, George Wills (1813–1893) from his Blackaller relations at Maidencombe. The author can remember the gleanies (guinea fowl) that used to roost in the tree, when any stranger approaching would be greeted with their cry 'go back!, go back!'

Narracombe in 1930, covered in roses and jasmine. The granite porch was added c.1850 and William Ball, Ilsington carpenter, said he remembered helping to build it.

The Farmhouse from the west side. This side was originally the longhouse building, two floors on the left sloping to a single storey cattle shed on the right.

A stark Narracombe after the front was replastered in 1956.

Left and below: *The old buildings at Narracombe were demolished in 1898 by my grandfather Charles Wills (1854–1921) in order to make way for a new range. The buildings are of typical design with shippens at the bottom and tallets above, with pigeon holes in the middle. The threshing barn stands on the right of the picture below – here grain was threshed using flails. The wall in the foreground still exists. The new range built on the site is of granite and the roof was of Bridgewater Roman tiles - these demanded by my grandmother who said she did not want to gaze out on a corrugated iron roof all day from the kitchen!*

Bottom: *Granite posts taken out of the old building in 1898 and used as a super clothes-line support.*

Below left: *This building was erected by my great grandfather, George Wills (1813–1893), in 1845. The ridge of the roof is not level but is parallel with the ground. The left-hand side was the pound house for pounding apples for cider, worked by a horse turning a wheel. On the right is the threshing floor. This is now a listed building.*

Narracombe farmyard. The circular granite trough came from the old pig's house and was used for feeding. The pigs tended to stand around the trough and not in it!

Narracombe pound house, a building on three levels, seen from the kitchen garden side. One of the first improvements made to the farm by the author's great-grandfather, George Wills, on his coming to Narracombe as a young man in 1836,

The corn chamber and cider cellar was built on the site of the former medieval 'Hall House' c.1702 and 'Cyder House' c.1728. This building was erected in the early 19th century and was formerly a cottage. It is referred to in Samuel Nosworthy's will of 1805 and was occupied by his two daughters, Sarah and Elizabeth, following his death. It was used as a cider cellar until c.1933 and then as a corn chamber until c.1935. The two annexes formed the wash-house and the trap-house or duck's-house. The upper storey is largely of cob.

Narracombe in 1954 surrounded on both sides by orchards.

Narracombe in 1975. By this time the expansion of the modern farm buildings had taken place with the sacrifice of the orchards.

Features of the interior at Narracombe include (left) the back door which is barred with a heavy length of wood instead of a lock; (centre) the turnspit in the kitchen which was used to mechanically turn meat on the spit over the fire by means of a variety of weights, ropes and pulleys. The author's Aunt Mary (1852–1937) told him that she recalled it being used in her early days. On the right is a dresser at Narracombe standing under one of the moulded oak beams which originally held up the platform in the living hall where the farmer and his wife slept. When the dresser was moved the outline of an ancient grandfather clock could be seen which, in its time, has also never been moved, and had been painted around.

NARRACOMBE PEOPLE

Above: *The author's three aunts with their pony, donkey, Sport the spaniel, and Twala the cat, 1908.*

Left: *Great Aunt Mary Wills and her sister-in-law, the author's grandmother, Amy Wills (1851–1931), picking primroses near Narracombe bridge.*

NARRACOMBE PEOPLE

William Harris of Plumley, Bovey Tracey (1804–1882), son of John Harris (1740–1834) and Mary Wills (1769–1823) of Town Barton, Ilsington.

Above: *The author's grand-mother, Polly Rendell (1858–1924), and uncle William (William F. Rendell 1891–1943).*

Right: *The author's mother, Mary Wills 1884–1974 (née Rendell), his uncle Francis Rendell, 1888–1967 and aunt Winnie Bartlett 1886–1968 (née Rendell).*

Above: *The author's mother, Mary Rendell), and (seated) his aunt Winnie. The Rendell family came from Combe-in-Teignhead, and later from Kingston House, Staverton.*

NARRACOMBE PEOPLE

The front of Narracombe in 1905 with the author's grandfather, Charles Wills, carrying his gun, and my aunts, May and Dolly, with my grandmother, Amy Wills (née Braim).

Above left: *Sydney George Braim Wills (1881–1947) under the Portugal laurel at Narracombe.* Centre: *Mrs Amy Wills, Sydney Wills, Charles Wills and young Charles Wills jnr, 1914.* Right: *Charles Wills who farmed Narracombe 1880–1911, and his grandson Charles Wills who farmed Narracombe 1930–1954.*

NARRACOMBE PEOPLE

Albert Giles, horseman at Narracombe for nearly forty years, with his son Reg.

EMILY BROWN - A NARRACOMBE CHARACTER

Emily Brown was what was called an assistant in the farmhouse at Narracombe when I was a small boy and she lived with us for some twenty years. Her family lived at Barracott at Manaton – an ancient farmstead under Easdon Down, occupied for years by the Nosworthy family, distant relatives of mine.

Barracott farmhouse had then been divided into two cottages and the Brown family lived in one of these. Emily Brown was a real old country character, full of superstitions and stories. One of these I remember well, was that one moonlit night she woke up and saw a boy wearing a tam-o-shanter hat standing beside her bed, silhouetted against the moonlight shining through the window. He walked across the room and disappeared into the cupboard. If one said to her that she must have imagined it her reply was 'Tis true I tell ee, I saw im as clear as I see ee now!' I wonder if he was a young Nosworthy!

Emily Brown had many sayings and, talking of a spinster who spent many years looking for her ideal husband, she used to say 'Er searched the orchard for the sweetest apple and picked a grab (a crab or sour apple) in the end! On winter evenings at Narracombe she would sit in front of a blazing hearth fire, knitting, with a cat on her lap. When anyone went into the kitchen she would say 'It's gwain to snaw, dawn't 'e 'ear the wind 'owling in the chimney?'

She was a very buxom woman and on winter afternoons would go out in the orchard or fields with a huge old fashioned cross-cut saw. This she used single handed and usually scorned any offer of help. She would saw off a huge log from a fallen tree, sometimes three feet in diameter and three feet long and roll this through the courtyard, through the back door and cross-passage into the kitchen hearth. Backed up with smaller sticks it would last for more than a week, and never needed re-lighting.

Sundays and Thursdays afternoons were her half-days. She would leave Narracombe about half past two and walk to Barracott seven miles away, whatever the weather. On reaching the moor at the top of Green Lane she would cut across the moor for about a mile to reach the Manaton road. She would reach home about five o'clock (unless she met someone to talk to on the way – she was a great talker) and would leave again about half past seven to be back at ten. Many times she lost the moor path in the mist, and one particularly dark night she dropped her torch and had to go on her hands and knees in the heather and bracken looking for it.

Another night, during the war, when black American soldiers were camped on the moor, a patrol stopped her in the middle of the moor and said 'Who goes there?' Emily Brown's maxim at night was 'Never speak to strangers, never look back and keep walking,' so she said nothing and continued on her way. The Yank shone his strong torch on her, and when he saw her said 'Pass on, sister!' She admitted afterwards that she was scared stiff.

Another very dark night her torch had nearly failed and when she was within three hundred yards of Narracombe she decided to cross a grass field as a short cut. This field had five gates to it, but once in the field she walked round and round trying to find the way out. She always maintained afterwards that she had been pixy-led. She firmly believed in pixies and ghosts.

NARRACOMBE PEOPLE

Far left: *The author's father, mother and two brothers, Sydney, Mary, Frank and Charlie Wills on the front lawn, 1917.*

Left: *Bill Derges, Dick Wills and Bill Cator with Caesar, at Narracombe in 1925.*

Below: *Georgie Wills with Crocket and Snowy, 1989.*

Above: *The three Wills boys, Frank, Charlie and Dick, on an island in the River Dart at Dartmeet, 1925*

Right: *A family gathering in the kitchen at Narracombe, 1995.*

16 - An Ilsington Farming Miscellany

George Northway cutting oats in Kilnclose field at Middlecott, 1954.

Left: Mavis Madge and Sam Courtier 'stitching up' sheaves of oats with the help of a little girl.

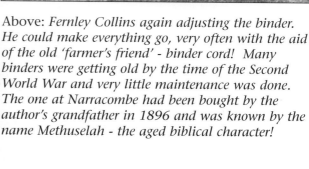

Above: *Fernley Collins again adjusting the binder. He could make everything go, very often with the aid of the old 'farmer's friend' - binder cord! Many binders were getting old by the time of the Second World War and very little maintenance was done. The one at Narracombe had been bought by the author's grandfather in 1896 and was known by the name Methuselah - the aged biblical character!*

Left: *Pete Collins, Brian Head and Fernley Collins, rabbiting.*

Right: *Sydney Wills and Bill Derges Snr standing up sheaves of corn.*

Below: *George Northway and Oliver Roberts starting build a corn rick at Middlecott.*

Below right: *Alan Ralph, Roy Frost and Jack Carpenter with their corn ricks at Narracombe, ready for the thatcher.*

Below: *One of the great skills of farming – thatching a rick. Here Joe Milton is seen atop a rick at Narracombe.*

Below right: *Corn ricks at Narracombe c.1958. Note that at this time the ricks were built in a rectangular shape, but the author recalls them (in the period 1925–45) being smaller and oval in shape, without any sharp corners.*

The following three pictures show the activity around the corn ricks after the arrival of the thrashing machine. Early thrashers were steam driven, later ones powered by tractors; the machines would be taken from farm to farm during the winter months. Sheaves from the ricks would be fed into the top of the machine and the grain extracted and put into large hessian sacks.

One or two men looked after the steam engine and the thrasher while the straw was fed down a moving conveyor (the reed comber), and either tied into bigger sheaves for feeding to animals or for bedding, or (in the case of the wheat straw in these photographs) tied into nitches of reed for house or rick thatching.

Thrashing was very labour intensive, as these photographs show. Ideally two men were needed to fork the sheaves from the rick to the top of the machine, two men to cut the binder cord and feed the sheaves into the thrasher, two men to handle the sacks of grain, two men to take the sacks to the granary, a man to pitch straw to another building the straw rick, and a doust boy to clear the 'dust' from under the machine.

Miss Blenkiron of Bagtor House and her donkey with some firewood to heat her home. Blacksticks, the stalks of gorse left after swaling, were gathered for lighting fires. Many old deeds of Ilsington cottages give a right of 'collecting blacksticks from the common.'

Arthur Courtier with his horse and cart near a snowy Haytor c.1950. Arthur was not to go over to tractor power until the mid 1950s.

Below: *Fred Saunders with his working horse.*

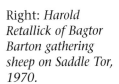

Above: *Norman Lampard (Classics Master at Chester Cathedral School) and George Rogers, retired farmer and Ilsington Churchwarden, returning after a day's sport with ferrets and rabbits.*

Right: *Harold Retallick of Bagtor Barton gathering sheep on Saddle Tor, 1970.*

Subscribers

John Adams, Emsworth
Ann Adams, Zeal Monachorum, Devon
Evelyn Adamson, Haytor, Ilsington, Devon
Beryl L. Alford, Liverton, Devon
Roy and Joy Anderson, Haytor, Devon
Mrs Dorothy Anfield (née Honeywill),
    Scarborough, N. Yorkshire
Mrs Muriel Ansted, Exeter, Devon
Ian D. Armitage, Beckenham, Kent
Tom and Shirley Arnott, Alton, Hants.
Ted and Marcella Ashman, Blackpool School,
    Devon
Tony and Sandy Ayliffe, Ilsington, Devon
Mark Baker, Bovey Tracey, Devon
W. J. Baker, Liverton, Devon
Julia A. Baker, Ilsington, Devon
Ern and Cynthia Baker, Haytor, Devon
Derek Barber, Hadleigh, Essex
David and Christine Bardell, Ilsington, Devon
E. J. Bashford, Penton, Cumbria
Andrea Baty, Hereford
Shirley J. Baty (née Grose), Kings Pyon,
    Herefordshire
David Bearne, East Lounston, Lounston, Devon
E. D. Bellis, Wickham, Hampshire
John D. Bewsher, Paignton, Devon
Mr Timothy Bidwell, Ilsington, Devon
Albert G. Blackwell, Liverton, Devon
Bill and Jean Blinston, Dartington, Totnes,
    Devon
Janice Bomford, Liverton, Devon
Oliver and Sarah Bosence, Ilsington, Devon
Jean Lesley Bowen-Brooks, Haytor, Ilsington,
    Devon
Peta and Pom Bradford, Tenterden, Kent
Panda Bradford, Brisbane, Queensland, Australia
Susan and Robert Bradshaw, Liverton, Devon
Brassley Family, Ilsington, Devon
Peter Jonathan Brecht, Charlottesville, Virginia,
    USA
David Charles Brecht, Boston, Massachusetts,
    USA
Stephen Frederick Brecht, Houston, Texas, USA
Amy Elizabeth Brecht, Texas, USA
Kath Brewer, Torquay, Devon
William F. Brewer, Bovey Tracey, Devon
David R. Briddock,
Virginia and Bill Brisco, St Albans, Herts.

Rosemary J. Brown, Ilsington, Devon
Stuart Browning, Bristol
Keith Bryant, Goodstone, Bickington, Devon
Muriel Bunclark (née Potter), Newton Abbot,
    Devon
K. J. Burrow, Bucks Cross, Devon
Colin and Liz Butler, Ilsington, Devon
Samuel Butler, Ilsington, Devon
Samuel Butler, Islington, London N1
Simon and Anna Butler, Manaton, Devon
Stephen Callard, Liverton, Devon
George and Molly Campbell, Haytor, Devon
Dennis L. Campion, Cheltenham, Glos.
The Campkin Family, Haytor, Devon
Alan Carpenter, Wrington, Somerset
Aileen and Peter Carrett, Exeter Cross, Liverton,
    Devon
Joyce Chandler (née Nosworthy), Braintree, Essex
Mrs N. Chapple (née Guest),
Richard and Jackie Chichester,
Vivienne Clare, Newton Abbot, Devon
Mrs Dawn R. Clark-Skinner, Newton Abbot,
    Devon
Alan and Nancy Cleave, Sigford, Devon
Miss Joyce Clifton, Haytor, Devon
Dawn E. Collinson, Ilsington, Devon
Vernon and Angela Coon, Liverton, Devon
Gary Cooper, Haytor, Devon
Robert Cornish, Liverton, Devon
Bob Cornish, Liverton, Devon
Nigel Cornish, Chatham, Kent
David Cornish, Liverton, Devon
Richard John Cornish, Ilsington, Devon
Nicholas Courtier, Canada
Margaret E. Courtier, Lancing, West Sussex
David Courtier, Canada
Roger Courtier, Haytor, Devon
Arthur and Lily Courtier, The Moors, Haytor,
    Devon
Gregory H. Courtier, Ashburton
John B. Courtiour, Bovey Tracey, Devon
Ethel Courtiour Rees, Frinton-on-Sea
Patricia A. Cox, Ilsington, Devon
Fiona Cox, Owlacombe Mine, Devon
Ada and Fred Cox
Robert and Maureen Dady, Liverton, Devon
Mr and Mrs Damgaard-Nielsen, Blueburn,
    Haytor, Devon

Dartmoor National Park Authority
Laurie and Lindsay Davidson, Haytor, Devon
Malcolm and Veronica Diggines,
    Liverton/Ilsington, Devon
Brian Ross Divett, East Horsley, Surrey
Carol and David Dixon, Liverton, Devon
Dr J. P. B. Dobbs, Haytor Vale, Devon
Mrs Anne Donaldson,
Ron and Barbara Douglas,
Mr and Mrs G. W. Dunn, Portland Villa,
    Ilsington, Devon
Bill and Marjorie Dymond, Liverton, Devon
David and Josephine Edge, Mill Brook, Liverton,
    Devon
Marion Edgecombe, Bovey Tracey, Devon
Heather and Bill Edwards, Ilsington, Devon
Ron Elms (Wills), Perth, Australia
Mr R. W. Evans, Ringwood, Hants
Ivan and Bridget Fincham, Brimley, Bovey
    Tracey, Devon
Mrs Barbara Fisher (née Ford), Wreningham,
    Norwich
Elizabeth Folland, Liverton, Devon
Tracey Fone, Ilsington, Devon
Martin Foster, Green Lane, Ilsington, Devon
Mrs Frances Fox, Haytor, Devon
Brenda E. French (née Rowell), Sutton, Surrey
Adrian Frost, Barnt Green, West Midlands
Roy Frost, Newton Abbot, Devon
Lottie Frost, Newton Abbot, Devon
Valerie Frost, Newton Abbot, Devon
Anne T. Gallant, Ramsey, New Jersey
Neil Gardner, Haytor
Rosemarie Gee, ex Trumpeter, Ilsington, Devon
Eric Gee, Bournemouth
Pamela George, Brimley, Devon
Patricia A. Gibson, Haytor, Devon
The Reverend Albert Ginno, Eastbourne, East
    Sussex
Revd Michael Glare, Shaldon, Devon
Pamela Govier, Ilsington, Devon
Marion Grant, Hampton, Middlesex
Joan Grant (née Honeywill), Tadworth, Surrey
J. and N. Green, West Stow, Suffolk
A. L. Green (Nosworthy), Harrow, Middlesex
Ronald W. Greenway, Liverton, Devon
Dr Tom and Mrs Elisabeth Greeves, Tavistock,
    Devon
Elizabeth Griffiths, Aberystwyth, Ceredigion
Garth Grose, Dean Prior, South Devon
Jenny Hackett, Stockland, Devon
Mary O. Haimes, Ilsington, Devon
Mr P. Hamilton-Leggett BSc, Tavistock, Devon
Elaine Hammond (née Baty), Malvern Link,
    Worcester

Timothy Divett Hancock, Crediton, Devon
Stuart and Margery Hands, Bickington, Devon
Joyce Southard Brecht Harlow, Houston, Texas,
    USA
William Hart, Lower Knowle, Lustleigh, Devon
Tim and Maura Hassell, Ilsington, Devon
Andrew J. Hawkins, formerly of Ilsington
W. J. Hearder, Bovey Tracey, Devon
Linda and Dennis Heasell, Sigford, Devon
Robert Hesketh, Bovey Tracey, Devon
Paul and Liz Hewitt, Ilsington, Devon
Catherine Hicks, Haytor, Devon
Geoff and Brenda Hill, Liverton, Devon
Dr and Mrs C. J. Hodgson, White Rock, British
    Columbia, Canada
Valerie Hodgson, Sheffield, S. Yorkshire
Mr and Mrs J. N. O. Hodgson, Ajax, Ontario,
    Canada
Mrs Eileen Hodgson (née Bickford), Ottawa,
    Ontario, Canada
Mrs V. J. Hollingsworth (née Border), York
John Honeywell, Hook, Hampshire
Cyril Honeywill, born Ilsington, Devon
E. M. Honeywill, Ilsington, Devon
Raymond J. Honeywill,
Derek A. Honeywill, Ilsington, Devon
Elsie M. Honeywill, Wellingborough, Northants
Beatrice M. Honeywill, Buckfastleigh, Devon
Mr Robin Hood, Torquay, Devon/Mem. Of Tom
    and Madeline Hood, Torquay
Paul and Helen Hughes, Ilsington, Devon
Alison Hunt, Haytor Vale, Devon
Susan J. Hunt, Westbury-on-Trym, Bristol
Mr and Mrs R. J. Hunt, Ilsington, Devon
Dulcie Hunter, Bagtor Mill, Ilsington, Devon
Josephine A. Inch (née Honeywill)
Denis C. Ingram, Co Durham
Tim and Ann Jenkinson, Liverton, Devon
Joy and Nick Jones, Haytor Vale, Devon
Mr Kenneth B. C. Jones, Ashburton, Devon
P. F. Joyce, Bovey Tracey, Devon
Bridget and Peter Kenyon
Mr Paul Kiddell, Norway
Colin C. Kilvington, Stoke, Plymouth, Devon
Mrs Juline Kingsley, Chudleigh Knighton, Devon
Mr K. Kirby OBE
Anthony J. Klinkenberg, Berkshire
Humphrey M. Klinkenberg, Gloucestershire
Christopher A. Klinkenberg, Lancashire
Connie and Peter Klinkenberg, Smallacombe
    Farm, Ilsington, Devon
Barry A. Lacey, Ilsington, Devon
Gerald and Christine Lamb, Ilsington, Devon
Mr L. S. Landon, Liverton, Devon
Jill Landrock (née Baty), Owslebury, Hampshire

Mike and Karen Lang, Woodstock, Liverton, Devon

Rt Hon Lord Monro of Langholm AEDL

Brian Le Messurier, Exeter, Devon

John and Kathy Lead, Bishops Waltham, Hants

Sam Leaman, Ilsington, Devon

George E. Leaman, Kingsteignton, Devon

Mrs Amy Lethbridge

Pamela B. Lind, Bovey Tracey, Devon

Mrs Beryl London, Exeter, Devon

Jonathan and Tania Lord, Haytor Vale, Haytor, Devon

Jeanne Southard Macomber, Lompoc, California, USA

Mr and Mrs Madge, Liverton, Newton Abbot, Devon

Mavis Madge, Haytor, Devon

Gavin Mair, Lewside, Ilsington, Devon

Anne Marie Mair, Ilsington, Devon

E. M. Mantell, Green Lane, Ilsington, Devon

Mr James Gordon Marriott

Win Marshall, Ilsington, Devon

Mrs Jenny Martin, Heathfield, Nr Newton Abbot, Devon

Jennifer Mason, Bovey Tracey, Devon

Mrs Audrey Matthews (née Ford), Teignmouth, Devon

A. G. Mc Cluskey, Haytor, Devon

Brian William Merchant, Liverton, Devon

Janine Mills, Sigford, Newton Abbot, Devon

Robert and Dianna Milne, The Sanctuary, Ilsington, Devon

Sylvia J. Miners, Chudleigh, Devon

Miss C. B. Montizambert, Ilsington, Devon

Mr and Mrs H. E. Moore, Haytor, Devon

Roy and Myrtle Morris, Ilsington, Devon

Brett Morrish, Ilsington, Devon

David John Morrish, Haytor Vale, Devon

Scott and Susana Morrish, Ilsington, Devon

Arch and Audrey Mortimore, Widecombe-in-the-Moor, Devon

Mrs Gloria Moss (née Collins), Fowey, Cornwall

Mr and Mrs S. Moulson, Liverton, Newton Abbot, Devon

Vanessa Moulson, Bovey Tracey, Newton Abbot, Devon

Daniel and Emily Muirden, Liverton, Devon

Kenneth Newall, Ilsington, Devon

Paul G. Northway, Ilsington, Devon

Hilary Novak, Ilsington, Devon

Mr N. J. Osborne, Westbury, Wiltshire

Mrs J. Osmond (née Squire), Middlesex

Sheila Palmer, Truro, Cornwall

Lewis and June Passow, Ilsington, Devon

Christine Pautsch

Richard J. Penellum, Liverton, Devon

A. C. (Tony) Perkins, Liverton, Devon

Janet E. Perkins, Totnes, Devon

John and Jennifer Perrin, Ashburton, Devon

Mrs M. J. Petherick (née Ford), Sydney, New South Wales, Australia

Mr David Phillips, Market Drayton, Shropshire

Mr and Mrs B. Philp, Honeywell, Ilsington, Devon

Lynette E. Pickering (née Lambshed), Eden Hills, South Australia

Mr and Mrs G. Pilkington, Ilsington, Devon

Mark Pool, Torquay, Devon

T. and P. M. Pool, Ilsington, Devon

Pamela J. Porter, Godalming, Surrey

Margaret Powell, Haytor Vale, Devon

Miss Mary E. Powlesland, Rochester, USA

Mr and Mrs Stuart Powlesland, Spreyton, Devon

Kevin M. Presland, Bovey Tracey, Devon

Maureen and Dennis Presland, Ilsington, Devon

Mrs Rosemary A. Price, Mere, Wiltshire

Audrey Prizeman, Plymouth, Devon

Michael J. A. Prowse, Fleet, Hampshire

Paul Marton Pugsley, Haytor Vale, Devon

Mr and Mrs D. W. Puttick, Eastbourne, Sussex

Joan I. Pyemont (née Stonelake)

Greg Ramstedt, Pleasant Grove, Utah, USA (Wills descendant)

Bill Ransom, Ilsington, Devon

Derek Sydney Reed, Dainton, Newton Abbot, Devon

Roger Retallick, Millcombe, Ilsington, Devon

Mrs Pauline M. Retallick, Ilsington, Devon

Russell and Carol Retallick, Bagtor, Ilsington, Devon

Stephen Roberts, Bargo, NSW, Australia

John Roberts, Bridford, Devon

G. S. Roberts, born Ilsington 1926

Christine, Lloyd, Jenna, Simon Roberts, Ilsington, Devon

Dr J. F. Robinson, London

Mr and Mrs Rolfe, Tamerton Foliot, Plymouth, Devon

Gaynor R. Rose (née Grose), Stalbridge, Dorset

Hannah Ruffles, Liverton, Devon

Michael Ruffles, Liverton, Devon

Sandra Ryan (née Hawkes), Basingstoke, Hants

Kathleen M. Sagar, Ilsington, Devon

Mike and Shirley Sanders, Bickington, Devon

Kieran E. Saunders, Newton Abbot, Devon

Mrs Fred Saunders

John K. Shapley, Orpington, Kent

Joyce Sharpe (née Milton), Old Town Hill

Mrs Jean Shephard, Peverell, Plymouth, Devon

Mike and Eileen Shippam, Ilsington, Devon

Geoffrey and Valerie Short, Ilsington, Devon
Gill and Sandy Simpson, Ilsington, Devon
Valerie Skedgel-Hill, Paignton, Devon
Mrs Hazel Skipsey, Burscough, Near South Port
Peter Smith
Karen and Doug Smith, Ilsington, Devon
Martin Smith, Liverton, Devon
Ken and Helen Smith
Mrs Linda J. Smith
The Smith Family, Pool Farm, Liverton, Devon
The Snook Family, Belle Vue, Liverton, Devon
John and Jane Somers Cocks, Abbotskerswell, Devon
Vivienne J. Soper, Pelham, Alabama, USA
Michael R. Squire
Margaret Ann Squire, Ilsington, Devon
Elizabeth Stearns, Radlett, Herts
S. M. Stephens, Ashburton, Devon
Ann and Geoffrey Stone, Higher Brimley, Devon
Mary E. Sutherland, Ann Arbor, Michigan, USA
Daphne and Peter Taylor, Bovey Tracey, Devon
Judy Taylor (Grose Family), Ashburton, Devon
Rt Hon. Lord Tebbit, CH
Mary E. Thomas, Ilsington, Devon
Andrew and Helen Thompson, Wokingham, Berkshire
Christine Thompson, Chiddingfold, Surrey
Joan M. Tiddy, Lewthorne, Ilsington, Devon
Jackie Wylie and Richard Tomlinson, Haymans Cottages, Liverton, Devon
Lindsay J. D. Towell, Bovey Tracey, Devon
Derrick and Joan Towell, Liverton, Devon
Brian Towell, Ilsington, Devon
Mrs Betty Tracy, Ilsington, Devon
Mr Hedley W. Upham, Langaller, Bovey Tracey, Devon
Mr Stewart J. Upham, Langaller, Bovey Tracey, Devon
Mr and Mrs R. A. Vane, Lincoln
Peter and Jean Vines, Chipley, South Knighton, Devon
Mr G. Waldron, Plymouth, Devon

John F. W. Walling, Newton Abbot, Devon
George and Yvonne Ware-Owen, Middlecott, Ilsington, Devon
Dorothy M. Warren, Liverton, Devon
Alan and Sheila Watson, Exeter, Devon
Mr and Mrs M. Watson, Haytor, Devon
Mr A. Watson, Exeter, Devon
Mrs Joyce Webber
Anne West, Haytor Vale, Devon
Ronald B. Westaway, Ilsington, Devon
Alan and Valerie Wheelhouse, Ilsington, Devon
Chris and Hazel White, Corbyns Brimley, Ilsington Parish, Devon
Malc, Sal, Tom, Russ and Jenny White, Haytor, Devon
Derek and Beryl White, Ilsington, Devon
The Whitehead Family, Ilsington, Devon
Michael G. Wiles, Smokey Lane, Ilsington, Devon
Mr and Mrs G. R. Wilkinson, Ilsington, Devon
W. Williams, Ilsington, Devon
Ed and Erica Williams, Ilsington, Devon
Ian James Wills, Montmorency, Victoria, Australia
William S. Wills, Belleville, Ontario, Canada
E. Michael Wills, Exeter, Devon
Mr Anthony Rendell Boyd Wills, Harpenden, Herts
Jim and Ruth Wills, New Milton, Hants
Anthony W. E. Wills, Farnham Common, Buckinghamshire
Michael John Wills, Lymington, Hampshire
Warren and Marilyn Wills, Nantucket Island, USA
Claire Wills-Shaw, Antioch, California, USA
Commander W.N.L. Woodley, OBE. RN
Mirja and Steven Woollard, Lower Lounston, Devon
Phoebe Wortley-Talbot, Haytor, Ilsington, Devon
Jack and Wynne Wrightson, Boys' Brigade, Haytor, Devon